THE SECESSION MOVEMENT
IN SOUTH CAROLINA
1847-1852

A Da Capo Press Reprint Series

THE AMERICAN SCENE
Comments and Commentators

GENERAL EDITOR: WALLACE D. FARNHAM
University of Illinois

The Secession Movement
in South Carolina
1847-1852

By Philip M. Hamer

DA CAPO PRESS • NEW YORK • 1971

A Da Capo Press Reprint Edition

This Da Capo Press edition of *The Secession Movement in South Carolina, 1847-1852,* is an unabridged republication of the first edition published in Allentown, Pennsylvania, in 1918. It is reprinted by permission from a copy of the original edition in the collection of the University of Virginia Library.

Library of Congress Catalog Card Number 75-124883

SBN 306-71036-6

Published by Da Capo Press
A Division of Plenum Publishing Corporation
227 West 17th Street, New York, N.Y. 10011

Manufactured in the United States of America

THE SECESSION MOVEMENT
IN SOUTH CAROLINA
1847-1852

UNIVERSITY OF PENNSYLVANIA

The Secession Movement in South Carolina, 1847-1852

BY

PHILIP MAY HAMER

A THESIS

PRESENTED TO THE FACULTY OF THE GRADUATE SCHOOL
IN PARTIAL FULFILLMENT OF THE REQUIREMENTS
FOR THE DEGREE OF DOCTOR OF PHILOSOPHY

H. RAY HAAS & CO.,
Printers and Publishers
ALLENTOWN, PA.
1918

PREFACE

The period, 1847-1852, forms but a small part of the more than thirty-five years during which may be traced the course of events which found its logical fulfilment in the secession of South Carolina from the Union in 1860. Although limited in time and, in this thesis, restricted largely to one state, the disunion movement of this period possesses a unity and significance sufficient to warrant separate treatment. In its first phase it was primarily a Southern movement in opposition to the attempted prohibition of slavery in the territories acquired as a result of the Mexican War. It developed under the leadership of John C. Calhoun into an effort to unite the South in a demand for the equality of the slave power within the Union or its independence without the Union. The difficulty of securing concerted action on the part of the slave holding states was demonstrated by the failure of the Nashville Convention, which, however, but for the Compromise of 1850, might have been, as Robert Barnwell Rhett believed it would be, "the beginning of a revolution."

In this first phase South Carolina had played an important but not too conspicuous part. In the second phase she openly demanded the rejection of the Compromise and the dissolution of the Union. Her disunion majority, however, was split into two factions: one demanding the secession of South Carolina alone from the Union; the other advocating disunion, but only in cooperation with other Southern states. The victory of the latter faction and the acceptance of the Compromise by the other states prevented any precipitate secession.

The failure of the secession movement left South Carolina in 1852 still within the Union, but rather from necessity than from choice. A decade earlier than the other states of the South she was convinced that negro slavery and the interests of the Southern states which were dependent upon that institution were threatened with destruction by a continuance of the political connection between the slave holding and the non-slave holding sections of the Union. That South Carolina did not secede in 1852, or even a year or two earlier, was due solely to the fact that she could not confidently expect even the cotton states to join her in the formation of a Southern confederacy. She remained within the Union until these states by 1860 had advanced to her position.

It is perhaps unnecessary to say that I have attempted to treat impartially this period in the history of my state. I cannot refrain, however, from expressing here my keen admiration for that handful of brave men who, led by Joel R. Poinsett, James Louis Petigru, and Benjamin F. Perry, in this period of extreme sectional hatred and partisan strife remained true and loyal defenders of the Union.

I wish to express my indebtedness to Professor W. K. Boyd of Trinity College at whose suggestion and under whose direction this study was begun. I am also indebted to Dean Herman V. Ames, under whose guidance the major part of my graduate work has been done, and to Professor A. E. McKinley, of the Graduate School of the University of Pennsylvania, for their reading and helpful criticism of the manuscript.

An article by Professor C. S. Boucher, "The Secession and Co-Operation Movements in South Carolina, 1848 to 1852," in the *Washington University Studies,* Vol. V, No. 2, appeared only after the completion of the manuscript of this thesis and has consequently been of no aid in its preparation.

P. M. H.

UNIVERSITY OF PENNSYLVANIA,
PHILADELPHIA, PA.
MAY, 1918

IV.

CONTENTS

v.

CHAPTER I

THE WILMOT PROVISO AND THE CAMPAIGN OF 1848

"Nullification has done its work," wrote James L. Petigru, a leader of the South Carolina Unionists, in 1833; "it has prepared the minds of men for a separation of the States, and when the question is mooted again it will be distinctly union or disunion." [1] Thirteen years later the United States was at war with Mexico, and the prospect of securing additional territory from that country led to the raising of the question which Petigru had foreseen. President Polk asked Congress for an appropriation of two million dollars to be used by him in securing an adjustment of the boundary with Mexico, and a bill for this purpose was introduced into the House. On August 8, 1846, David Wilmot, of Pennsylvania, precipitated the sectional conflict by moving as an amendment to this bill a proviso prohibiting slavery in any territory that might be acquired from Mexico. [2] The House accepted the proviso and passed the bill thus amended, but the session came to an end before a vote could be taken in the Senate.

In South Carolina little attention was paid at first to the proviso. A few of the newspapers were mildly alarmed. The Camden *Journal* [3] saw indications of a coming struggle which would convulse the Union; the Greenville *Mountaineer* [4] feared that territorial conquests would raise issues vital to the exist-

[1] J. L. Petigru to H. S. Legare, July 15, 1833, in J. B. Allston, "*Life and Times of James L. Petigru,*" in Chas. *Sunday News,* June 3, 1900.

[2] *Cong. Globe,* 29 Cong., 1 Sess., 1217.

[3] Quoted in Pendleton *Messenger,* Oct. 16, 1846.

[4] Oct. 30, Nov. 13, 1846.

ence of every Southern state; and the Pendleton *Messenger*,[5] re-
puted to be Calhoun's organ, though at first inclined to dismiss
the Wilmot Proviso with the opinion that it would have failed in
the Senate and ought to have done so, declared a little later, in
view of the general disposition of both parties in the North to
court the abolitionists, that beyond the Missouri Compromise
line the South would not yield an inch.   These were but scat-
tered warnings.   Even in the South Carolina legislature, which
was in session during November and December, 1846, the question of slavery extension into the territories caused no discussion.

Congress reassembled in December, and within the next few
weeks it became clear that the principle of the Wilmot Proviso
had received the indorsement of the people of both parties in
the North and would be insisted upon by their representatives
in Congress.   The realization of this caused alarm in the South.
The gravity of the situation appeared so great to John C. Calhoun, senator from South Carolina and foremost champion of
slavery, that he wrote: "What is to come of all this, time only
can disclose.   The present indication is, that the South will be
united in opposition to the Scheme.   If they regard their safety
they must defeat it even should the Union be rent asunder....
We never had a darker or more uncertain future before us."[6]
Yet Calhoun thought that the contest would not arise until the
expected territory should actually be acquired.   This likewise
was the view of South Carolina's most influential state rights
paper, the Charleston *Mercury,* which declared that the South
would firmly insist upon her fair share of the proposed acqui-
sition.[7]

[5] Aug. 21, Nov. 13, 1846.

[6] Calhoun to Mrs. T. G. Clemson, Dec. 27, 1846, *Calhoun Correspondence,* 716.

[7] *Mercury,* Dec. 24, 1846.

A settlement of the question of slavery in the territories along the line of that made by the Missouri Compromise would, at this time at least, have been satisfactory to South Carolina.[8] But the defeat of an amendment to the Oregon territorial bill, proposed by Representative Burt of South Carolina, which would have committed Congress to this principle,[9] and the adoption by the House for the second time of the Wilmot Proviso,[10] convinced the press of the state that any division of the spoils of war between the two sections would not willingly be granted by the North. A storm was brewing, they warned their readers, which would shake the Union to its centre; the Republic was in danger; the ruin of the South had been decreed, and she must be prepared to meet the issue.[11]

Calhoun had been "waiting for developments." On February 19, 1847, four days after the House had adopted the Wilmot Proviso for the second time, he presented in the Senate his views on the question at issue in the form of a series of resolutions prefaced by a speech in which he denounced the proviso and called upon the South to resist. His resolutions, soon termed "The Platform of the South", were as follows:—

"*Resolved,* That the territories of the United States belong to the several States composing this Union, and are held by them as their joint and common property.

"*Resolved,* That Congress, as the joint agent and representative of the States of this Union, has no right to make any law, or do any act whatever, that shall directly, or by its effects, make any discrimination between the States of this Union, by

8 Chas. *Evening News,* quoted in Pendleton *Messenger,* Jan. 29, 1847; Greenville *Mountaineer,* Jan. 22, 1847; Pendleton *Messenger,* Jan. 22, 1847; *Mercury,* Feb. 20, 1847.

9 *Cong. Globe,* 29 Cong., 2 sess., 187.

10 *Ibid.,* 425.

11 Pendleton *Messenger,* Jan. 1, 1847; Chas. *Evening News* quoted in *ibid.,* Jan. 15, 1847; *Mercury,* Dec. 24, 1846, Feb. 9, 24, 1847.

which any of them shall be deprived of its full and equal rights in any territory of the United States acquired or to be acquired.

"*Resolved,* That the enactment of any law which should directly, or by its effects, deprive the citizens of any of the States of this Union from emigrating, with their property, into any of the territories of the United States, will make such discrimination, and would, therefore, be a violation of the Constitution, and the rights of the States from which such citizens emigrated, and in derogation of that perfect equality which belongs to them as members of this Union, and would tend directly to subvert the Union itself.

"*Resolved,* That it is a fundamental principle in our political creed, that a people, in forming a constitution, have the unconditional right to form and adopt the government which they may think best calculated to secure their liberty, prosperity, and happiness; and that, in conformity thereto, no other condition is imposed by the Federal Constitution on a State, in order to be admitted into this Union, except that its Constitution shall be republican; and that the imposition of any other by Congress would not only be in violation of the Constitution, but in direct conflict with the principle on which our political system rests." [12]

Calhoun did not press his resolutions to a vote as he had planned. The principles they asserted were intended to form the constitutional basis for Southern opposition to the Wilmot Proviso, and for this purpose the presentation of the resolutions in the Senate was sufficient. A few days after their introduction the Senate rejected the Wilmot Proviso; the House receded from its position; and the adjournment of Congress postponed for the time being the threatened sectional conflict. There could be no doubt, however, that the effort to prevent the further ex-

[12] Calhoun, *Works,* IV, 348; *Cong. Globe,* 29 Cong., 2 sess., 455.

pansion of slavery would be renewed. The speeches of Northern representatives in Congress, the agitation of the question in the newspapers of the North, and the approval of the Wilmot Proviso by the people of the non-slaveholding states, expressed in the resolutions of public meetings and of state legislatures, were sufficient evidence of this.

On the side of the South the first state to take an official position was Virginia. On March 8, 1847, her legislature adopted resolutions which expressed, even to a certain extent in the same words, the doctrine of Calhoun's resolutions regarding the rights of the states in the territories. In addition they asserted the determination of the people of Virginia, should the adoption and attempted enforcement of the Wilmot Proviso force the issue upon them, determinedly to resist ''at all hazards and to the last extremity.'' They called upon every man, in every section of the country, if the Union were dear to him, to oppose the passage of the proviso; and, in the event of its passage, they urged every slaveholding state and all citizens thereof, as they valued ''their dearest privileges, their sovereignty, their independence, their rights of property, to take firm, united and concerted action in this emergency.'' [13]

In South Carolina the newspapers vigorously denounced the Wilmot Proviso, and urged the South to speak out in defense of her rights. As was to be expected, the resolutions of Calhoun and of Virginia met with a decided approbation. On the evening of March 9th, an enthusiastic meeting of the citizens of Charleston was held to welcome Calhoun who was in the city on his way home from Washington. The resolutions adopted by the meeting reiterated verbatim the Virginia resolutions; asserted that the question at issue was paramount to all considerations of party and temporary policy; and declared that

[13] *Laws of Virginia,* 1846-47, 236; H. V. Ames, *State Documents on Federal Relations,* 245-247.

submission to the proposed exclusion of slavery, beyond what had already been yielded by the Missouri Compromise, "would be unwise, dangerous, dishonorable, and debasing." A report accompanying these resolutions expressed the conviction of the citizens of Charleston that the developments of the past year required "the most grave and earnest consideration of the whole people of the slaveholding States." The introduction of the Wilmot Proviso and its acceptance by the House in August, 1846, the passage by the House of the Oregon bill without the Missouri Compromise and with the Wilmot Proviso, the second passage of this proviso in the House during the last session of Congress, the whole temper of the Northern press, both Whig and Democratic, in sustaining this action, and the resolutions of the legislatures of nine Northern states denouncing slavery and protesting against its further extension, convinced them of the fixed determination on the part of the non-slaveholding states that slavery was not to be allowed to exist in any of the territories of the United States and that no other slave state would be admitted to the Union. The report furthermore asserted that slavery must be preserved or the South would be ruined, and that to preserve slavery the South must jealously watch her rights under the Constitution, insist upon her proportionate influence intended by the compromises of that compact, and above all must maintain at all hazards her equality in the Union. [14]

Calhoun, addressing this assembly, declared it his conviction that a large majority of both parties in the non-slaveholding states were determined to appropriate to themselves all existing and future territories of the United States. Anti-slavery sentiment, he said, was growing, and he was convinced that unless the South met the issue promptly and decidedly, the two sections

[14] Calhoun to Duff Green, Mar. 9, 1847, and to T. G. Clemson, Mar. 19, 1847, *Calhoun Correspondence*, 718, 720; *Mercury*, Mar. 10, 1847.

of the Union would soon become so thoroughly alienated that no
course would be left to the South but abject submission to abolition or a severance of the bonds of the Union.   The action that
he urged upon the South was the destruction of all party dis-
tinctions and the formation of one Southern party having as its
sole object the defense of slavery.   Such a party Calhoun believed would hold the balance of power in the nation, be able
then to put a stop to anti-slavery agitation, and thus save slavery and save the Union. [15]

Though Calhoun not only hoped but expected that the slavery agitation would break up the old party organizations, [16] the
time for this had not yet come.   Outside of South Carolina both
parties were strong, and while the proposal of a Southern party
met with some approval, the majority of the people of the South
considered the existing party system sufficient for the protection
of Southern interests.   Even within South Carolina, where the
Whig party was insignificant and Calhoun's influence was paramount, there were some who realized that the formation of a
Southern party on the slavery issue would force the North to do
the same and thereby destroy those bonds of party which yet
aided in holding the two sections together.   Calhoun they suspected of presidential aspirations, and his Charleston speech
they privately declared to be a bid for the vote of the South.
Ex-Governor James H. Hammond, nullifier and long an advocate of disunion, feared that outside of South Carolina this
would be so clear that ''our cause'' would be thrown back.   Virginia has started the ball, he wrote to William Gilmore Simms,
and, as the state best able to rally the South and lead to victory,
she should be kept in the lead.   ''South Carolina under present

[15] Calhoun, *Works*, IV, 382-396.
[16] Calhoun to T. G. Clemson, July 8, 24, 1847, *Calhoun Correspondence*,
735, 736.

auspices,'' he continued, ''can do nothing if she puts herself foremost but *divide the South* and insure disastrous defeat.'' [17]

During the summer of 1847 Calhoun's friends in Charleston directed their efforts towards arousing the South. An extra edition of the *Mercury* containing the Wilmot Proviso, the resolutions of ten Northern states favoring it, the Virginia resolutions and the Charleston resolutions opposing it, and a leading editorial by Franklin H. Elmore, President of the South Carolina State Bank, was widely distributed in the slaveholding states. Efforts were made towards the establishment of a Southern press at Washington. Letters and subscription lists, soliciting support for this enterprise, were circulated, but except from Charleston and its vicinity little financial aid was received. [18] The *Mercury* took the lead in the newspaper agitation and urged the South to make clear to the North its determination to meet the issue, should it be presented, on the forum or on the battle field. [19] The agitation directed from South Carolina was not without its effect. Throughout the South various papers began to take alarm, and the old proposal of a Southern convention was again advanced. It was not, however, until a number of papers in various Southern states had urged the assembling of such a convention that the *Mercury*, wisely having thought it best ''that the initiative for the attainment of this great object should be taken by others,'' gave its specific approval to the suggestion. [20]

Calhoun, in his private correspondence, was doing his part

[17] Hammond to Simms, Mar. 21, Apr. 1, 1847; Simms to Hammond, May 1, 1847, Hammond MSS.

[18] H. W. Conner to Calhoun, Aug. 23, 1847, *Calhoun Correspondence*, 1128; I. W. Hayne to James H. Hammond, Mar. 31, 1847; I. W. Hayne to Soule, Aug. 25, 1847; A. P. Aldrich to Hammond, Aug. 30, 1847, Hammond MSS.

[19] *Mercury*, Aug. 9, 1847, and issues of August and September, *passim*.

[20] *Ibid.*, Sept. 30, 1847.

to promote unity at the South in defense of slavery. In this connection it is important to note his opinion of the question of slavery in the territories as expressed in a conversation with President Polk in December, 1846. He agreed with Polk that slavery probably never would exist in the territories that were to be acquired from Mexico. He further stated, if Polk's account may be accepted as correct, that he did not desire to extend slavery, but that the attempt to prohibit slavery in the territories would involve a principle against which he would vote. [21] Calhoun evidently changed his mind about the possibility of the existence of slavery in the South-west, and he certainly did desire its extension, for the fact that the Northern section of the union was outstripping the Southern was his chief grievance and the chief cause for his fear that the South would soon be unable to protect slavery within the Union. But it is true that he attached less importance to the Wilmot Proviso *per se* than numerous others who took part in the Southern movement of this period. At least he took a broader view of the controversy between North and South; he considered the Wilmot Proviso but one of the numerous issues affecting slavery which should be settled; and he looked more to the ultimate political than economic results of its adoption. It is not too much to say that the introduction of the Wilmot Proviso gave to Calhoun the opportunity of forcing the whole issue of slavery upon the North. If he had not desired it and did not welcome it, at least he was not slow in seizing it.

Nothing makes clearer the position that Calhoun took in 1847, and furnishes a better key to an understanding of his activities and his purposes during the next three and final years of his life, than a letter he wrote at this period to a member of the Alabama legislature. In reply to a request for his opinion as to

[21] James K. Polk, *Diary*, II., 283-284.

what steps should be taken to guard the rights of the South, Calhoun wrote: ''I am much gratified with the tone and views of your letter, and concur entirely in the view you express, that instead of shunning, we ought to court the issue with the North on the slavery question. I would even go one step further, and add that it is our duty—due to ourselves, to the Union, and our political institutions, to force the issue on the North. We are now stronger relatively than we shall be hereafter, politically and morally. Unless we bring on the issue, delay to us will be dangerous indeed......Such has been my opinion from the first. Had the South, or even my own State backed me, I would have forced the issue on the North in 1835, when the spirit of abolitionism first developed itself to any considerable extent. It is a true maxim, to meet danger on the frontier, in politics as well as war. Thus thinking, I am of the impression, that if the South acts as it ought, the Wilmot Proviso......may be made the occasion of successfully asserting our equality and rights, by enabling us to force the issue on the North......But in making up this issue, we must look far beyond the Proviso. It is but one of many acts of aggression, and, in my opinion, by no means the most dangerous or degrading, though more striking and palpable......With this impression, I would regard any compromise or adjustment of the Proviso, or even its defeat, without meeting the danger in its whole length and breadth, as very unfortunate for us. It would lull us to sleep without removing the danger, or materially diminishing it.'' The letter then continued with a denunciation of the personal liberty laws of Northern states, and anti-slavery agitation in all its phases. Coming to the consideration of how the whole question could be met ''without resorting to a dissolution of the Union,'' a measure which should be used only as a last resort, Calhoun proposed retaliation on the part of the South by a refusal to fulfill the constitutional stipulations in favor of the Northern states.

Specifically he suggested the exclusion of Northern ships and commerce from Southern ports. To give force to such measures and to make up the issue, he urged a convention of the slaveholding states. [22] The idea of commercial retaliation was similarly urged upon his Charleston friends, in a letter to them approving the plan then under consideration, but soon temporarily abandoned, of organizing the South into Southern Rights Associations. [23]

While Calhoun was thus considering the measures that should be adopted by a Southern convention, in South Carolina a further impetus to the agitation against the Wilmot Proviso was given by public meetings held in all sections of the state. The first of these, at Edgefield Court House early in September, adopted the Virginia resolutions and expressed a willingness to cooperate with the Southern states in averting injustice and resisting aggression. [24] A meeting at Darlington on October 4th declared that the South should make no concession beyond the Missouri Compromise line; it deemed the Union as dust in the balance if its preservation required submission to the Wilmot Proviso; and it demanded that the Southern representatives in Congress, upon the adoption of this proviso, leave their seats and return home. [25] In Anderson a resolution was adopted urging the South Carolina legislature to request the representatives of the state in Congress to retire from their seats, should the proviso pass, and return home to consult regarding measures

---

[22] This letter, without date and without the name of the addressee, is given by Benton in his *Thirty Years View*, II, 698-700. Extracts, with minor changes in wording, also printed in J. W. DuBose, *Life of Yancey*, 200-201. For the idea of forcing the issue, *cf.* J. H. Hammond to W. G. Simms, Nov. 17, 1848, ''The Wilmot Proviso issue as I told you at the first was the weakest of all we could have made the fight on.'' Hammond MSS.

[23] Letter dated Sept. 28, 1847, published in *Mercury*, May 5, 1851.

[24] Hamburg *Journal*, quoted in Pendleton *Messenger*, Sept. 24, 1847.

[25] *Mercury*, Oct. 11, 1847.

for the protection of the slaveholding states. [26]   The people of
Laurens professed a devotion to the Union, but at the same time
pledged resistance to the Wilmot Proviso "although a dissolution of the Union be the result." [27]   A Greenville meeting adopted resolutions substantially those of the Virginia legislature. [28]
The planters of Edisto Island declared for "resistance in the
most effective mode," [29] and those of Georgetown pledged their
cooperation in such defensive measures as aggression should
compel. [30]

    Though for the most part these meetings, of which the above
are representative, were unanimous in demanding resistance to
the Wilmot Proviso, few of them outlined any definite measures
of resistance.   And when they advocated resistance by the
united South, they did not specifically outline the means by
which this might be accomplished.   But a meeting on November
2nd in Pickens District, in which was located Fort Hill, Calhoun's home, made definite and elaborate proposals, save as to
the final action to be taken should all other action fail.   Calhoun
apparently took no part in the proceedings, but the resolutions
adopted express exactly his position at this time.   They denounced not only the Wilmot Proviso but also the action of
Pennsylvania and other Northern states in preventing the execution of the fugitive-slave law, and they proposed action by the
South along three general lines.   They urged first, the removal
of party considerations, the establishment of a Southern press
at Washington, opposition to any presidential candidate not
openly opposed to the Wilmot Proviso, the refusal to enter into
caucus or convention with those favorable to the proviso, and the

[26] *Ibid.*, Nov. 16, 1847.
[27] Greenville *Mountaineer*, Oct. 29, 1847.
[28] *Ibid.*, Oct. 8, 1847.
[29] *Mercury*, Nov. 8, 1847.
[30] *Winyah Observer* (Georgetown), Nov. 10, 1847.

calling of a convention of the Southern states to unite the South
for common action along these lines. In the event of the failure
of these milder measures they proposed a second step—the setting aside of the constitutional provisions favorable to the Northern states and epecially the exclusion of their ships and commerce from Southern harbors. Should this likewise fail, the
resolutions of this meeting declared, ''we stand prepared to
throw the responsibility on our assailants, and take the final remedy into our own hands, without fear that we in the end will be
the greatest sufferers.'' [31]

In the up-country one of the most active leaders in opposition
to the Wilmot Proviso was Benjamin F. Perry. In nullification
days Perry had been a Unionist. Because of this fact and because of his later opposition to secession, his attitude towards
the proviso is worthy of careful notice. In a speech at the
Pickens meeting he declared that the question raised by the Wilmot Proviso was one of life or death, and that its passage would
be ''tantamount to a dissolution of the Union.'' Out of the country to be acquired from Mexico perhaps ten or fifteen states
would be formed, and the effects of the Wilmot Proviso, he
thought, would be to draw a cordon of free states about the slaveholding country, cut off all outlet for property in slaves, and
make that property, as it increased, valueless and a fatal nui-
sance to the South. Perry was speaking in that district of South
Carolina which contained the smallest proportion of slaves and
the greatest proportion of non-slaveholders of any district in the
state. The men assembled at this meeting did not perhaps feel
themselves vitally interested in the question of slavery extension, but they did possess their full share of prejudice against
the black race. To this prejudice Perry directed an appeal frequently met with in the speeches delivered in this section of the

[31] Pendleton *Messenger,* Nov. 12, 1847.

state. He declared that the avowed spirit of abolition was to make the negro not only free "but the equal of his master.... He is to go with him to the polls and vote, to serve on juries, appear in court as a party and a witness. He is to meet the white man as an equal and visit his family, inter-marry with his children and form one society and one family!" To defeat this spirit of abolition in the North and to save the Union the speaker proposed that a convention of the slaveholding states be held during the coming winter. It would show to the North the real temper of the South on this question, he thought, and exert a controlling influence on congress. "Let them speak firmly, coolly and dispassionately," he said, "and declare that any interference on the part of the Federal Government with slave property will be the cause of an immediate dissolution of this great and hitherto glorious Union....The voice of a single State may not be heeded but when the whole South speaks, her admonition will and must be respected." [32]

Waddy Thompson was one of the few South Carolina Whigs. Speaking in Greenville from the same platform with Perry he declared to the audience before him: "The alternatives before you are in my deliberate judgment, resistance at all hazards and to every possible extremity, to this insulting, degrading and fatal measure [the Wilmot Proviso], or the conversion of the South into black provinces." Being a Whig, Thompson hoped to avoid the issue by refusing to acquire territory from Mexico. But should the issue come, "What then is the remedy?" he asked. "There is but one....That word is not used in the Resolutions which have been submitted, but the thing is meant—Dissolution. Gentlemen, I ask you, in the event of the assertion of the principle of the Wilmot Proviso by the act of Congress, are you ready to dissolve the Union? I am." [33]

[32] *Ibid.*, Dec. 10, 17, 1847.
[33] Greenville *Mountaineer*, Oct. 15, 1847.

South Carolina had as yet taken no official stand on the question which by now had so aroused her people. Her legislature met in annual session late in November. In his message to that body Governor David Johnson discussed the question of the Wilmot Proviso at some length but in moderate tones, and he recommended the Virginia resolutions as a correct expression of the rights of the slaveholding states and as pointing to the proper action. [34] In the Senate, resolutions reported by the Committee on Federal Relations were unanimously adopted. [35] The first four were in substance, and in part verbatim, the Virginia resolutions. The fifth, however, was in advance of the position taken by Virginia. It declared that in the event of the passage by Congress of a law prohibiting the introduction of slave property into any territory acquired from Mexico or from any other power, it would become the duty of the governor of South Carolina to convene immediately the legislature in order that it might take such actions as should by it be deemed necessary and becoming; and it requested that the Governor, between the summoning and assembling of the legislature, "correspond and consult with the authorities of other states with a view to harmonious action on this important subject." [36] In the House, meanwhile, the Committee on Federal Relations, having considered a number of resolutions on the Wilmot Proviso, reported for adoption the Virginia resolutions verbatim. [37] On the last day of the session the House considered the Senate resolutions and asked leave to amend by striking out the fifth. This request the Senate refused to grant. A conference committee failed to reach any agreement, whereupon the House tabled the Senate

---

[34] *S. C. House Journal*, 1847, 19-20.
[35] *S. C. Senate Journal*, 1847, 130-131.
[36] *Courier*, Dec. 16, 1847.
[37] Columbia *Daily Herald*, Dec. 14, quoted in *Courier*, Dec. 16, 1847.

resolutions and adopted without roll call just before adjournment the Virginia resolutions as reported by its committee. [38]

The reasons for the failure of the two houses to agree upon
the stand that South Carolina should take were not explained at
the time. The two sets of resolutions illustrate a division of
opinion as to the course South Carolina should take, which was
more or less present during the whole period of the Southern
movement resulting from the introduction of the Wilmot Proviso. Both houses were, of course, in favor of the sentiments expressed by the Virginia legislature as far as they went. The
Senate resolutions represented the opinion of those, impatient of
delay and of restraint, who desired that the state go beyond
Virginia and assume a position requiring some definite action.
But this was in conflict with the opinion of wiser leaders who
sought union of opinion and of action by the South, and who
realized that this could better be obtained with Virginia rather
than South Carolina in the lead.

Already the Virginia resolutions had met with a favorable
response in other states. In May, 1847, the Alabama Democratic Convention had given them its approval, [39] and a few
weeks later the Georgia Democracy did the same. [40] Governor
Brown of Mississippi declared that they met a hearty response in
his state from both parties. [41] In December the Alabama legislature adopted resolutions which not only took the position of
Calhoun and Virginia that the territories were the common
property of the states and protested against the prohibition of
slavery in them, but declared it the duty of Congress to protect
slave property within the territories. They promised, more-

[38] *S. C. House Journal,* 1847, 205, 206, 207, 208. Neither of the resolutions is given in the *Journals* or in the *Reports and Resolutions,* and
hence the citations to newspapers.
[39] *Niles' Register,* LXXII, 179.
[40] *Ibid.,* 293.
[41] *Ibid.,* 178.

over, that Alabama would act in concert, and make common
cause, with the other slaveholding states, for the defense, in any
manner that might be necessary, of the institution of slavery. [42]
The Texas legislature on February 2nd, 1848, declared the proposed prohibition of slavery in the territories unconstitutional,
and on March 18th, asserted that the state would not submit to
such restriction if applied to any territory that might be acquired from Mexico. [43]   In the other Southern states no official
action was taken, and the presidential campaign soon absorbed,
for the time being, practically all attention.

In South Carolina General Taylor had early been looked
upon with some favor as a presidential possibility. [44]   The *Pendleton Messenger*, as early as May 28, 1847, while urging that
South Carolina should keep aloof from the campaign until
further developments, declared that should Taylor later come
out as a free trade man and decline a caucus nomination it might
become the duty of the state to support him. [45]   In Charleston
the feeling in favor of Taylor was very strong, but on the advice of Calhoun it was for the time being kept quiet. [46]   There
was even some hope on the part of Calhoun's friends that he
would be able to take the field as an independent candidate, [47]
but the futility of this hope made any action in that direction
impossible.   Cass, as one of the leading candidates for the Democratic nomination, was highly objectionable because of his advocacy of the right of the people of a territory to settle for themselves the question of slavery.   This doctrine of "squatter sovereignty" had been advanced by Senator Dickinson of New York

[42] *Laws of Alabama*, 1847-48, 450-451.

[43] 30 Cong., 1 sess., *House Misc. Doc.*, Nos. 27 and 91.

[44] Hammond to W. G. Simms, Apr. 19, 1847, Hammond MSS.

[45] Pendleton *Messenger*, May 28, 1847.

[46] H. W. Conner to Calhoun, Dec. 8, 1847, *Calhoun Correspondence*,
1147.

[47] James Gadsden to Calhoun, Dec. 9, 1847, *ibid.*, 1148-1149.

in resolutions presented to the Senate, December 14, 1847, [48] and
approved by Cass in his Nicholson letter of December 24. [49] Calhoun was in close touch with the *Mercury* and he was interested
in seeing that this paper properly noticed Dickinson's resolutions. [50] This the *Mercury* did without much prompting, and in
its own vivid style denounced the doctrine of squatter sovereignty, and condemned all of its advocates as men who desired to
seem to abandon the Wilmot Proviso and yet retain its principle. [51] In the Senate Calhoun denied that either the people or
the legislature of a territory had a constitutional right to exclude slavery. [52] Yet some sentiment favorable to this settlement of the question existed within the state and increased with
the progress of the presidential campaign. [53]

Acting on the advice of Calhoun, [54] yet contrary to the
wishes of a considerable element who thought that the state
should take some action in common with the other Southern
states and no longer content herself with protestations, South
Carolina, as previously in 1840 and 1844, took no part in the
Democratic Convention which met in Baltimore the latter part
of May. [55] Her avowed reason for thus remaining aloof was

[48] *Cong. Globe*, 30 Cong., 1 sess., 27.

[49] *Niles' Register*, LXXIII, 293.

[50] Henry Gourdin to Calhoun, Jan. 19, Feb. 4, 1848, *Calhoun Correspondence*, 1159-1161.

[51] *Mercury*, Jan. 6, 17, Feb. 2, 11, 1848.

[52] Speech on the Oregon Bill, June 27, 1848, Calhoun, *Works*, IV, 498.

[53] D. J. McCord to Hammond, Jan. 9, 1848, Hammond MSS. Compare
the editorials of the *South Carolinian*, Feb. 15 and June 23, 1848, for attitude on squatter sovereignty before and after the nomination of Cass.

[54] H. W. Conner to Calhoun, Apr. 13, 1848, *Calhoun Correspondence*,
1166-1167.

[55] One Democrat from South Carolina attended the convention and was
given the right to cast all of the votes of the state. The *Mercury* declared
that his representation of the state was a farce, his only title to representation being election by a meeting of fifty-five persons at Georgetown,
among whom was "*one solitary planter* (the delegate himself), in the midst
of a population of planters, nearly all Democrats." *Mercury*, May 26,
30, 1848.

that she feared to compromise her position by taking part in proceedings which might result in the nomination of a candidate whom she could not support. [56] The chief organ of the radicals demanded of the convention as the price for the state's support, the nomination of a man "true and above taint or suspicion," true to those constitutional principles "on the maintenance of which hangs the fate of slavery—the welfare of the Slave States —the existence of the Union." [57]

The Democratic Convention, however, nominated Cass and Butler, and rejected by a large majority the extreme pro-slavery resolutions proposed by Yancey, of Alabama, demanding protection by the United States of slavery in the territories and denying to the inhabitants of the territories the power to prohibit it. The *Mercury* declared the nomination of Cass very unsatisfactory. [58] A meeting of the Charleston Democrats on June 6th denounced the proceedings of the Baltimore Convention as "unsatisfactory and objectionable," but it tabled as premature resolutions nominating General Taylor, and decided to await developments before expressing any preference for the presidency. [59] Taylor's acceptance of the Whig nomination left the Democrats of South Carolina more than ever undecided as to whom they should give their support. The situation was rather fittingly expressed in a toast offered at a Fourth of July celebration in Saint Paul's Parish: "General Cass and General Taylor: the two horns of a dilemma to Southern patriots. We want no statesman who has knuckled to abolitionists, or who marches under the banner of Whiggery. Yet if compelled to elect will prefer the advocate of a Tariff to the approver of the Wilmot Proviso." [60]

[56] *Ibid.*, May 20, 27, 1848.
[57] *Ibid.*, April 24, May 20, 1848.
[58] *Ibid.*, May 30, June 2, 1848.
[59] *Ibid.*, June 7, 1848; *Courier*, June 7, 1848.
[60] *Mercury*, July 8, 1848.

A distinct division of sentiment on the course South Carolina should pursue soon became apparent. On July 20th, the
situation was cleared somewhat by a meeting in Charleston of
Taylor Democrats. These declared themselves under no obligation to support the nominee of the Democratic Convention
''whose opinion, on a subject to them of paramount importance,
has been marked by singular vacillation;'' and they concurred
in the nomination of General Taylor ''made by the people of
the United States, irrespective of parties, and independent of
politicians.'' Fillmore, however, they could not accept; and
W. O. Butler, the regular Democratic nominee, was named as
their choice for the vice-presidency. [61] In other districts Cass
and Taylor meetings were held, and the state was soon in the
midst of a heated and somewhat bitter campaign. On August
21st a Cass and Butler meeting in Charleston, held contrary to
the advice of Calhoun, [62] condemned Whig latitudinarianism
and its ''whole brood of Federalist measures,'' and expressed
its preference for Cass because he was a Democrat and also because he was opposed to and denied the constitutionality of congressional legislation on the matter of slavery. [63] On the same
day the *Mercury,* after a long period of hesitation, came out for
Cass, [64] having concluded, that though Cass had not given all the
pledges that were desired, Taylor had given none, and that the
friends of Cass at the North were more favorable to the South
than were the friends of Taylor. [65] Calhoun remained neutral.
In both candidates he saw much to condemn and little to ap-
prove, and desired to be regarded as taking no part between the

[61] *Ibid.,* July 21, 1848.
[62] J. M. Walker to Hammond, Aug. 22, 1848, Hammond MSS.
[63] *Courier,* Aug. 22, 1848.
[64] *Mercury,* Aug. 21, 1848.
[65] *Ibid.,* Aug. 5, 1848.

two, but as standing ready to support or oppose the successful as his measures might or might not accord with his own. [66]

As presidential electors were chosen by the legislature, the only method by which the people of the state could express their preference between the presidential candidates was in the choice of legislators who had pledged themselves for Cass or for Taylor. In Charleston the contest seems to have been the most hotly contested. Here, as well as in some other districts and parishes, both Cass and Taylor tickets were named. The elections, which occurred October 9th and 10th, resulted in a victory for the partisans of Cass. Charleston, with the aid of the small Whig minority, it was alleged, [67] elected a Taylor man to the United States Congress, a Taylor man to the State Senate, and thirteen Taylor and four Cass Democrats to the House. [68] The legislature, called into special session for the purpose, chose Cass electors by a vote of 129 to 27. [69]

[66] Calhoun to editor of the *Mercury*, Sept. 1., 1848, published in *ibid.*, Sept. 6, 1848.

[67] *Mercury*, Oct. 23, 1848.

[68] *Ibid.*, Oct. 13, 1848.

[69] *S. C. House Journal*, extra sess., 1848, 11.

CHAPTER II

UNITED ACTION URGED, 1848-1849

Contrary to the expectations of the Whigs,[1] the temporary division in the ranks of the South Carolina Democrats did not prove permanent. Calhoun and other leaders sought to prevent a bitterness in the campaign which would divide the state and weaken her position in opposition to the aggressions upon slavery. For a time the campaign had tended to distract attention from all other questions, but even before it was over the still unsettled question of slavery in the territories was pushed to the front.

In August, speaking in Charleston, Calhoun urged moderation and kindly feeling in the conduct of the campaign, for he thought that the time was soon to come when the united energies of the South would be needed for the struggle with the growing spirit of abolition. He still clung to the idea that a Southern party might enable the South to command her own terms in cooperation with a party in the North. ''But,'' he continued, ''if this fails to arrest the spirit of aggression now so manifest, and the alternative is forced upon us of resistance or submission, who can doubt the result. Though the Union is dear to us, our honor and our liberty are dearer. And we would be abundantly able to maintain ourselves. The North is rich and powerful but she has many elements of division and weakness.... The South, on the contrary, has a homogeneous population, and a common

---

[1] Robert Toombs to John J. Crittenden, Sept. 27, 1848, *Toombs, Stephens and Cobb Correspondence*, 128; ''Charlestonian'' to N. Y. *Courier*, in *Mercury* Oct. 25, 1848.

bond of union, which would render us powerful and united.
Wherever Southern men have been placed upon the battlefield
.....they have shown themselves in generalship and soldiership
at least equal to those of any other section of the Union.   Our Custom Houses would afford us a revenue ample for every purpose.
....In whatever aspect, then, we consider it we will be as well
prepared for the struggle as the North." [2]

Never had Calhoun spoken so openly of the possibility of
disunion.   Heretofore, South Carolina had protested and threat-·
ened but, restrained by Calhoun, her citizens had for the most
part refrained from an advocacy of any specific plan of action
which would have placed the state in advance of the others of the
South.   The idea of a Southern convention had been suggested
as early as the fall of 1847, and as we have seen, Calhoun had
written with this object in view to some of his supporters outside of South Carolina.   But in the opinion of one of these, the
people of no state, save South Carolina, were then ready for such
action, [3] and the occasional suggestion of a Southern convention had failed to arouse any enthusiasm.   Concerted action by
the South was now demanded generally throughout South Carolina.   Representative Burt, a close friend of Calhoun, recommended a convention of slave holding states as the only means
whereby the South could save herself from the ultimate destruction of slavery. [4]   A meeting of the citizens of Saint Peter's
Parish, September 9, recommended the call of a Southern convention and the adoption, if necessary, of "startling measures"
to preserve the honor, liberty, lives and property of the South,

[2] *Mercury*, Aug. 21, 1848. Calhoun found it impossible to write out his
remarks in full, but considered this report of his speech as good as could be
expected. See his letter to the editor, in *ibid.*, Sept. 6, 1848.

[3] Wilson Lumkin to Calhoun, Nov. 18, 1847, *Calhoun Correspondence*,
1135-1139.

[4] Speech at Abbeville, Sept. 4, Abbeville *Banner*, Sept. 9, quoted in
Mercury, Sept. 12, and Greenville *Mountaineer*, Sept. 15, 1848.

and belligerently declared the proper forum for debate on the Wilmot Proviso, "the field of battle, where our muskets can be the orators, powder and ball the argument." [5]

The meeting which attracted most attention, however, and whose resolutions seem to have met with the greatest approval, was that of Fairfield District, held at Winnsboro Court House, November 6. The first resolution declared that the effort to exclude the Southern states from the territories was calculated to degrade them and ultimately to destroy slavery "by circum-scribing its limits and rendering it valueless;" that such exclu-sion would be a gross violation of the constitution, and "must tend to sever the bonds of the Union." The second characterized the passage of the Oregon territorial bill with the prohibition of slavery, "a gratuitous insult to the South." The third pro-tested against the injustice of the Missouri Compromise, but ex-pressed a willingness to acquiesce in its extension to the Pacific "as a final settlement of the question." The fourth resolution expressed attachment to the Union but declared it "unworthy of preservation when it shall cease to serve the great end and ob-ject of its creation—'to secure equal rights and equal privileges to all'." The fifth declared the preference of the meeting for a Southern convention or concerted action by the legislatures of the states as the most effectual remedy, yet claimed for South Carolina, should the other states decline to act in concert with her, the right to determine for herself the extent of her griev-ances as well as the time, mode and measure of redress. Finally, the sixth resolution declared that the passage by Congress of the Wilmot Proviso or any similar measure, or "the submission by Congress to such action on the part of the territories them-selves south of 36° 30'," would be cause for decided action on the part of the whole South; and it authorized the immediate

[5] *Mercury,* Sept. 20, 1848.

representative of Fairfield district in Congress in such event to vacate his seat and return home.

The Fairfield meeting also appointed a committee of twenty-one to correspond throughout the South and endeavor to bring about concert and harmony of action. This committee, of which John H. Means was chairman, issued a few weeks later an Address to the South in which it declared that nothing short of the entire manumission of all slaves and the elevation of them to political equality with their masters would ever satisfy the North, and urged that "self-respect, the safety of our institutions, our duty to posterity, all summon us to resistance, and should the bonds of the Union be shattered into atoms, let not the sin rest upon us, but upon those who by a long series of indignities, have goaded us into madness." [6]

The newspapers of the state were almost unanimous in urging resistance. The *South Carolinian* (Columbia) demanded that the South "show her enemies that whilst we sustain the Union in a spirit of justice and even compromise, we will never consent to remain in it as the oppressed bearers of burdensome exactions, and forever be harassed by unjust and unholy attacks upon our prosperity and institutions." The *Palmetto State Banner* urged the South to prepare for the contest, "even though that contest be one of death and blood." The Sumter *Banner* hoped that South Carolina would take the lead in organizing a Southern convention to pledge the South to equality in the Union or secession from it. The *Spartan* and the Pendleton *Messenger* urged approval of the Fairfield resolutions by other districts. The Abbeville *Banner* advocated resistance to the proposed re-

[6] Proceedings of the Fairfield meeting, in *Mercury*, Nov. 16, 1848, and *South Carolinian*, Nov. 14, 1848. "Address of the Fairfield Committee of Correspondence to the South," in *ibid.*, Feb. 27, 1849, and *Spartan*, Mar. 6, 1849.

striction of slavery in the territories "if needs be at a sacrifice of the Union." [7]

Even allowing for all possible discount of these and similar violent outbursts, it is quite apparent that there existed in South Carolina a determination to resist the application of the Wilmot Proviso to the territories recently acquired from Mexico—at least to that part of them south of 36° 30'. But as to the mode of resistance and even as to the wisdom and desirability of much agitation in South Carolina on the question, there was some difference of opinion. Calhoun worked now, of course, for united Southern action by means of a convention of the slave-holding states. He probably realized at this time, as his later activity in this respect clearly indicates, and others certainly did, that any precipitate action on the part of South Carolina, any attempt at assumption of leadership by her, would be detrimental to the end he had in view. In Charleston, the Taylor Democrats induced their opponents who had favored Cass to join with them in advocacy of united action on the part of the South, and appointed a committee of correspondence to work for this result. It was their desire "to fan the flame" and get some other state to lead off, but they went about it with caution. Charleston was not the state, and any definite proposal from the state was not desired. [8]

However, it was difficult at times to hold all in line. It was feared that there was danger of a serious attempt at state action on the part of some ambitious and impatient leaders in the state, and it was partly to forestall and prevent such a movement that the meeting of the Taylor men in Charleston was held

[7] These and others quoted in *Mercury*, Oct. 13, Nov. 21, 1848.

[8] *Mercury*, Nov. 2, 1848; *Courier*, Nov. 2, 1848; H. W. Conner to Hammond, Nov. 2, 20, 1848; Hammond to Simms, Nov. 17, 1848; Simms to Hammond, Nov. 24, 1848; Hammond MSS. See also Minority Report at the Fairfield meeting, *South Carolinian*, Nov. 14, 1848.

and its resolutions adopted. [9] The Fairfield platform contemplated separate action by South Carolina should the other
Southern states fail to join with her, and other expressions
looking to this remedy were sufficient to warrant some alarm.

The most outspoken advocate of independent action was
Robert Barnwell Rhett. He had made a speech in Charleston on
September 23, in which he demanded less talking and more action. "Meet the question at once and forever," he said...."bring
your power to bear directly on the question—not through a
Southern Convention which you cannot get (and which if you
get, may only breed confusion and weakness in the South) but
by the States......Let the Southern States instruct their Senators and request their Representatives, to leave their seats in
Congress immediately and return home, should abolition in any
of its forms prevail in the legislation of Congress....and the
South is safe. But if the South still sleeps inactive, submissive
to aggressions—if no other state will maintain her dignity and
her rights under the Constitution on this great question, let
South Carolina, unaided and alone, meet the contest. She can
force every state in the Union to take sides, for or against her.
She can compel the alternative—that the rights of the South be
respected, or the Union be dissolved." [10] To Rhett's position the
Mercury gave its support in December. While willing to try a
Southern convention, it thought the plan impossible, and declared: "Separate State action, we believe to be the only means
of redress, and there is but one state, which, by its unanimity,
is able properly to begin and enforce this remedy. That state is
South Carolina." [11]

[9] Chas. *Evening News*, quoted in *Mercury*, Nov. 21, 1848; W. G. Simms
to Hammond, Nov. 11, 1848, Hammond MSS.; H. W. Conner to Calhoun,
Nov. 2, 1848, *Calhoun Correspondence*, 1184-1185.
    [10] *Courier*, Sept. 29, 1848; *Mercury*, Sept. 29, 1848.
    [11] *Ibid.*, Dec. 11, 1848.

The South Carolina legislature, meeting in November, was called upon to set forth officially the position of the state. Governor David Johnson devoted about one-fourth of his message at the opening of the session to a consideration of the slavery question. Throughout it was moderate in tone, and the recommendations therein made met the very decided approval of the conservative element in the state. [12] The time for action, he thought, would not arrive until the question of slavery in the territories should be settled against the South. Until such a time had arrived it could not be expected that either the friends of Polk, before his administration had expired, or the friends of Taylor, after the inauguration of the new administration, would be willing to act in anticipation that the rights of the South would be invaded, for each believed that the presidential veto would be used against the Wilmot Proviso.. Yet every contingency ought to be provided for, and no time lost in projecting means to unite the slaveholding states in common action when the occasion should arise. Free discussion and interchange of opinion would greatly promote this object. No state acting alone in opposition to the opinion of all others could hope for success. Unity of time and concert of action were indispensible, and a Southern convention, the governor thought, was the best means of obtaining this. [13]

In the legislature resolutions expressing sentiments in accord with those of the governor were introduced. [14] Some members, however, desired a bolder stand and proposed, that, in the event of the exclusion of slavery from the territories south of the line 36° 30', the representatives and senators in Congress from South Carolina should vacate their seats and the legislature of

[12] *Courier*, Nov. 30, 1848.
[13] *S. C. Senate Journal*, 1848, 26-28.
[14] *S. C. Senate Journal*, 1848, 46; *House Journal*, 1848, 96-97.

the state be summoned to take the necessary action. [15]   These
resolutions indicated the differing views of those who looked to
other states for leadership in concerted action and those who
wished independent action and leadership by South Carolina.
However, none of these resolutions were brought to a vote.   Calhoun was in Columbia on his way to Washington and was invited
to a seat on the floor of the legislature. [16]   It can hardly be
doubted that the action taken by the legislature was in perfect
accord with his wishes.   A joint committee on federal relations
reported the following resolution which was adopted, after protest on the part of some few who still desired prompt and vigorous action, [17] by the unanimous vote of both houses:

"*Resolved, unanimously,* That the time for discussion, by
the slaveholding states, as to their exclusion from the territory,
recently acquired from Mexico, has passed; and that this General Assembly, representing the feelings of the State of South
Carolina, is prepared to cooperate with her sister states in resisting the application of the principles of the Wilmot Proviso
to such territory, at any and every hazard." [18]

In Congress the hostility to slavery was growing. The Clay-
ton Compromise, which Calhoun supported, had failed in the
House, and the Senate had been forced to accept the Oregon
territorial bill stripped of its extension of the Missouri Compromise line to the Pacific. Early in the second session of the Thir-
tieth Congress, the House instructed the committee on territories to report a bill for the organization of New Mexico and
California and excluding slavery therefrom. [19]   On December 21,
it adopted a resolution instructing the committee on the District

---

[15] *S. C. Senate Journal,* 1848, 13, 39; *House Journal,* 1848, 95.
[16] *S. C. Senate Journal,* 1848, 61; *South Carolinian,* Dec. 8, 1848.
[17] *Mercury,* Dec. 14, 1848.
[18] *S. C. Reports and Resolutions,* 1848, 147.
[19] *Cong. Globe,* 30 Cong., 2 sess., 39.

of Columbia to bring in a bill for the prohibition of the slave trade within the District. [20]   This action caused great excitement among the Southern members who met in caucus the following evening and appointed a committee to prepare an address to the people of the Southern states.   This action resulted in the adoption, January 22, of a document drawn up by Calhoun and only slightly modified by the caucus, "The Address of the Southern Delegation in Congress to their Constituents."   It was signed, however, by only two Whigs and forty-six Democrats, and was supported by the unanimous delegations of only two states, Mississippi and South Carolina. [21]

The Southern Address began with a resume of the slavery question in the United States since the formation of the Constitution, and attempted to point out the growing hostility to and increasingly dangerous aggressions upon slavery.   It declared that if aggressions were not promptly met and ended, that if by the prohibition of slavery in the territories, the free states were permitted soon to number three-fourths of the United States, the abolition of slavery would be the result.   To prevent this the address urged union among Southerners in placing the slavery question above all others.   It concluded: "If you become united and prove yourselves in earnest, the North will be brought to a pause, and to a calculation of the consequences; and that may lead to a change of measures, and the adoption of a course of policy that may quietly and peaceably terminate this long conflict between the two sections.   If it should not, nothing would remain for you but to stand up immovably in defense of rights, involving your all—your property, prosperity, equality, liberty and safety." [22]

[20] *Ibid.*, 84.
[21] Hearon, *Mississippi and the Compromise of 1850*, 38-39; W. M. Meigs *Life of Calhoun*, II, 426-431.
[22] Calhoun, *Works*, VI, 290-313.

On January 20, 1849, two days before the Southern Address was issued, the Virginia legislature adopted a new set of resolutions. These reaffirmed the position taken two years previously, and in addition they declared that the abolition by Congress of slavery or the slave trade in the District of Columbia would be a direct attack upon the institutions of the Southern states to be resisted at every hazard. They furthermore advanced Virginia to a position not yet assumed by any other Southern state, by requesting the governor, in the event of the passage by Congress of the above mentioned objectionable legislation or of the Wilmot Proviso, immediately to convene the legislature "to consider the mode and measure of redress."[23] In Florida, also, the legislature pledged the state to join the other Southern states "in taking such measures for the defense of our rights.....as the highest wisdom of all may, whether through a Southern Convention or otherwise, suggest and devise."[24] Even the Whig legislature of North Carolina adopted resolutions, noticeably pacific in tone nevertheless, declaring unjust and unconstitutional the abolition of slavery or the slave trade in the District of Columbia and the prohibition of slavery in the territories, and advocating the extension of the Missouri Compromise line to the Pacific.[25] Missouri also expressed a willingness for such a settlement, and declared her readiness to cooperate "with the slaveholding states in such measures as may be deemed necessary for our mutual protection against the encroachments of northern fanaticism."[26]

In South Carolina, public meetings in practically every district and parish gave prompt and emphatic endorsement to the Southern Address and to the resolutions of Virginia, Florida

[23] *Laws of Virginia*, 1848-49, 257.
[24] Jan. 13, 1849. 30 Cong., 2 Sess., *Sen. Misc. Doc.*, No. 58.
[25] Jan. 27, 1849. 30 Cong., 2 Sess., *House Misc. Doc.*, No. 54.
[26] Mar. 10, 1849. 31 Cong., 1 Sess., *Sen. Misc. Doc.*, No. 24.

and North Carolina. They professed a willingness on the part of the people of South Carolina to cooperate with the Southern states, and declared that unless a firm and united stand were taken disunion or abject submission to wrong would soon become the only alternative. But they did not insist that this was now the only alternative, and, for the most part, they did not propose that any definite action be taken by South Carolina. The chief advance beyond previous positions was the taking of the first steps in organization for resistance. In most districts and parishes Committees of Safety and Correspondence were appointed, charged with the duty of reconvening the meetings when it should be deemed necessary and of conducting correspondence with other similar committees in South Carolina and other states for the purpose of devising proper measures for their common safety. [27]

The next and obvious step after local organization had been made was soon taken. A Kershaw District meeting, held March 3, at Camden, adopted a resolution requesting the various committees of Safety and Correspondence to send delegates to a meeting in Columbia, for the purpose of devising and recommending to the people of the state a system of non-intercourse in trade and commerce with the non-slaveholding states. [28] The idea of non-intercourse met with little encouragement at this time, [29] but two days later a Sumter meeting requested its Committee of Safety to invite similar committees of other districts to send delegates to Columbia for the purpose of organizing a Central Committee of Safety. The duties of this committee should be to meet as often as necessary, to correspond with similar committees in other states and with the district committees of South Carolina, and, should the occasion require, to take measures for

[27] See *Mercury,* and *Courier,* Feb.-Apr., 1849, *passim.*
[28] *Mercury,* Mar. 9, 1849.
[29] See, however, *South Carolinian,* Mar. 13, 16, 1849.

the convening of the people of South Carolina with the view of promoting "firm, united and concerted action" at the South. [30] Acting on these suggestions, the Richland Committee of Safety and Correspondence some weeks later invited the several district committees to send delegates to a meeting in Columbia to be held the second Monday in May. [31]

Calhoun's opinion as to the action the meeting should take was of course solicited. Non-intercourse he now objected to as neither dignified, nor prudent, nor efficient. He thought that the great object of the meeting should be the adoption of measures to prepare the way for a convention of the Southern states, but what these measures should be the meeting could best decide. He did suggest, however, that the organization of South Carolina and the other Southern states was an indispensable step, and for that and other purposes there ought to be appointed a central committee. [32]

One hundred and nine delegates from twenty-nine districts and parishes met in Columbia May 14, and organized with the election of ex-Senator D. E. Huger as chairman. The various proposals regarding the action the meeting should take were submitted to a committee of twenty-one. This committee on the following day reported resolutions which were unanimously adopted. These were moderate in tone as compared with the press and many of the district meetings, and represent, so far as ascertainable, the deliberate opinion at this time of the people of the state. The first, for this reason, may well be quoted in full:

"*Resolved,* That full and deliberate examination of the whole subject has forced a deep conviction on the Delegates of

[30] Sumter *Banner* quoted in *Mercury,* Mar. 10, 1849.
[31] *Tri-weekly South Carolinian,* Apr. 10, 1849.
[32] Calhoun to John H. Means, Apr. 13, 1849, *Calhoun Correspondence,* 764-766.

the Committees of Safety here assembled from the several Districts and Parishes of the State, that alarming and imminent peril is hanging over the institutions and sovereign rights of the slaveholding states, caused by unconstitutional and mischievous interference with our domestic slavery and the rights of slaveholders on the part of the people of the North, their Legislatures, Courts, and Representatives in Congress, and by withholding from them the aids and remedies guaranteed by the Constitution. The arguments and appeals to cease and abstain from this course of unprovoked wrong and insult, have been exhausted in unavailing efforts, which have only been followed by repetitions of injury, and aggressions more alarming, persevered in with an appearance of concert and determination, which leaves to us no alternative but abject and humiliating submission, or a like concert and determination in maintaining our constitutional rights and in defending our property and persons thus wantonly put in danger. That South Carolina should stand prepared, as she now is, to enter into council, and take that 'firm, united and concerted action' with other Southern and South Western States in this emergency, which the preservation of their common honor, sovereignty and constitutional privileges demands, and to maintain them at every hazard and to the last extremity—and, that in view of this alarming condition of public affairs, a Central State Committee of Vigilance and Safety, to consist of five members, be now raised by ballot, to correspond with other Committees and persons in this and other States with a view to such concerted and united measures as may be expedient in any emergency that may arise.''

Other resolutions approved the Southern Address, and concurred in the Virginia resolutions twice adopted by the legislature of that state, ''feeling and believing that......the liberties, honor and interest of the slaveholding states will be safe under her lead.'' And in the language of one of the Virginia resolutions of 1849, they called upon the governor of South Carolina, in the event of the passage of the Wilmot Proviso or any other measure abolishing slavery or the slave trade or admitting slaves to vote in the District of Columbia, to convene the legislature to consider the mode and measure of redress. The meeting also recommended that the districts and parishes preserve and perfect the organization of their committees "for the purpose of correspondence and concert of action, and especially exert themselves to spread useful information before the people, and to detect and bring to justice all offenders against our peace and institutions." In accordance with the first resolution a central committee of five was appointed, consisting of F. H. Elmore, Chairman, Wade Hampton, D. J. McCord, James Gadsden, and F. W. Pickens. [33]

The work of this meeting was decidedly conservative. It had been urged that some definite action be taken by it, at least to the extent of devising some plan of resistance looking ultimately to a separation of the Union, and of inviting the other Southern states to cooperate with South Carolina in this plan. [34] While the meeting expressed a willingness on the part of South Carolina to enter into council and take joint action with the other Southern states, it did not address itself to them or issue any invitation for a common conference to consider joint action.

For some months after this meeting South Carolina was apparently very quiet. There was an almost total and very sudden cessation of inflammatory editorials and but few contributors to the newspapers aired their views on the question at issue. That there was some dissatisfaction with the proceedings of the meeting of delegates from the Committees of Safety was evi-

[33] The proceedings of this meeting are published in the Greenville *Mountaineer*, May 25, and the *Mercury*, May 15, 16, 17, 1849.

[34] *Tri-weekly South Carolinian*, Apr. 21, 1849; resolutions of Sumter Committee of Safety, in *ibid.*, Apr. 21, 1849.

denced only by one meeting, in Sumter County, which protested
against the indecision and apparent tameness of that body and
declared that not only should a Southern convention have been
urged but the time and place set for its assemblage. [35] But if
this feeling was at all extensive, it found exceedingly little expression. Governor Seabrook traveled throughout the state, re-
viewing the militia and telling them that they might soon be
called upon to defend their homes, [36] but the press of the state
made little reference to his activities. It appeared that those
who dictated the opinions of the press and the policy of the
state desired that South Carolina should keep quiet while events
which they desired developed elsewhere. Outwardly, the state
was calm, but the leaders within the state were at work.

The governor's activities were not clear, but they indicate
attempts on his part to secure some measure of military pre-
paredness on the part of the state. On June 6, he issued a circular letter to the Major-Generals of the state militia, asking
them to summon a board of officers to consider the defects of the
militia system and the measures necessary for remedying them;
the expediency of reestablishing brigade encampments; the ad-
visability of erecting buildings for the keeping of arms and am-
munition; and finally what steps ought to be taken by the state
to meet any emergency that might arise. [37] General D. Wallace
of the fourth district reported as regards the last question, that
the existing system was sufficient neither for the preservation
of domestic peace nor for any emergency that might arise from
"foreign invasion." He recommended that a body of about
seven thousand well-armed minute men be created to serve as a
nucleus about which the citizen soldiery could rally. He approved the governor's measures to put not only Charleston but

[35] *Tri-weekly South Carolinian,* Aug. 11, 1849.
[36] Correspondence of N. Y. *Herald,* quoted in *Mercury,* Oct. 22, 1849.
[37] *S. C. Reports and Resolutions,* 1849, 420-421.

the whole state in a position for effectual defense. [38]   Thirty thousand dollars were spent by the governor in the purchase of arms. [39]   The Central Committee interested itself in the defenses of Charleston and conferred with the governor on the subject, but it is not apparent what actual steps were taken. [40]

[38] *Ibid.*, 451-453.
[39] Message to the legislature, *S. C. Senate Journal,* 1849, 23.
[40] F. H. Elmore to Seabrook, May 30, 1849, Seabrook, MSS.

CHAPTER III

THE NASHVILLE CONVENTION

While agitation had ceased in South Carolina, the movement for Southern resistance gathered headway in the other cotton states and led ultimately to the assembling of a convention of the Southern states. South Carolina had been ready for some months to support this movement and a call for such a convention could easily have been secured from her. It was desirable, however, that some other state take the lead in this movement and to this end Calhoun had been directing his efforts. His recommendation of a Southern convention, made during the few preceding years to various friends and supporters throughout the South, had not produced the desired results. More than two years of almost continuous agitation of the slave question in and out of Congress better prepared the South for the united stand that Calhoun desired. The Southern Address, despite the fact that it failed to receive the support of almost all the Whigs and many of the Democrats in Congress, had its effect. Mississippi, of all the Southern states save South Carolina, was more thoroughly aroused and more nearly united on the question of resistance, and in this state, under the direction of Calhoun, the movement for a Southern convention was formally launched.

Several months of agitation in Mississippi resulted in a meeting of the citizens of the central part of that state at Jackson, May 7, 1849. Representing only a small portion of the state the meeting did not feel authorized to prescribe any course of action. It therefore recommended that for this purpose a convention of all the people be held in Jackson the first Monday in October; and it proposed that delegates to this convention, divided equally between the two parties, be chosen by primary meetings of citizens in each county. [1]

The proceedings of this meeting were sent to Calhoun by Collin S. Tarpley, a prominent leader of the Mississippi movement, with the request for his opinion as to what course should be adopted by the October convention. Calhoun replied that in view of the fixed determination of the North to push the abolition question to the last extreme, there was but one promise of saving both the South and the Union—a Southern convention. The great object of this convention, he wrote, should be to issue an address to the other states, setting forth the causes of Southern grievances and admonishing them as to the consequences if they should not be redressed, "and to take measures preparatory to it, in case they should not be. The call should be addressed to all those who are desirous to save the Union and our institutions, and who, in the alternative, should it be forced upon us, of submission or dissolving the partnership, would prefer the latter. No state could better take the lead in this great conservative movement than yours. It is destined to be the greatest of sufferers if the Abolitionists should succeed; and I am not certain but by the time your convention meets, or at furthest your Legislature, that the time will have come to make the call." [2] To Senator Foote of Mississippi who likewise had asked for advice, Calhoun wrote in the same strain, urging that the October convention make the call for a Southern convention—to save the Union if possible, but at all events to save the South. [3] That the Mississippi Convention would act upon this suggestion was promised Foote by leaders of both parties in his state. [4]

---

[1] Hearon, *Miss. and the Compromise of 1850*, 46-50.

[2] Calhoun to C. S. Tarpley, July 9, 1849, quoted by Foote in a speech in the Senate, Dec. 18, 1851, *Cong. Globe*, 32 Cong., 1 sess., appx., 52.

[3] Calhoun to Foote, Aug. 3, 1849, *Mercury*, June 4, 1851.

[4] Foote to Calhoun, Sept. 25, 1849, *Calhoun Correspondence*, 1204.

In the meantime Governor Seabrook of South Carolina and the Central Committee of Vigilance and Safety had been sounding out official sentiment in other Southern states relative to that cooperative resistance which they so ardently desired and in which South Carolina was fully prepared to join. With the approval of the Central Committee the governor wrote in May to a number of the Southern governors, outlining the impending danger to Southern institutions and Southern rights and inquiring as to what degree of cooperation could be expected from their states in measures of resistance and defense. [5] Unfortunately the character of the replies cannot be determined save that received from Governor Moseley of Florida who, though unable to warrant cooperation by his state because of the opinions of his Whig successor, soon to assume office, and the none too hostile feeling of many towards the Wilmot Proviso, yet hoped and felt convinced "that Florida would cordially and promptly cooperate with Virginia and South Carolina in any measure that those two States would *decisively adopt* and *energetically pursue* in defense of a common institution and sovereign dignity." [6] At any event it was decided to send a confidential agent to Mississippi to be present at the convention at Jackson in October, and for this commission Daniel Wallace, Representative in Congress, was chosen. [7] Missions to other states probably were considered

[5] Elmore, Chairman of the Central Committee, wrote to Seabrook, May 30, 1849, "I do not now see any other Executive to whom to address yourself besides those you have already approached." Seabrook MSS. The nature of Seabrook's letters is derived from the reply of the governor of Florida, endorsed, "Confidential letter from Gov. Moseley of Florida May 18, 1849." *Ibid.*

[6] Moseley to Seabrook, *op. cit.*

[7] "Letter from Hon. D. Wallace accepting this confidential appointment to go to Jackson, Mississippi. June 8, 1849" to Seabrook. Seabrook MSS.

and may have been sent, [8] but if so, the reports on them have not yet been discovered.

The Mississippi Convention met on the appointed day with most of the counties of the state represented. Calhoun's letters were shown to some of the leaders "well up to Southern rights," but acting upon the generally accepted opinion that only failure could result from a course known to have been recommended from South Carolina, these leaders endeavored to keep secret from the majority of the members of the Convention and from the general public Calhoun's connection with the movement they publicly inaugurated. [9] General Wallace was surprised at the extent of hostility towards and suspicion of anything thought to be of South Carolinan origin. He "was told by some gentlemen in private that if South Carolina *had attempted to lead,* in the struggle for southern rights, the result would have been disastrous for the cause. The Democrats were driven to their utmost skill, to keep the Whigs in the right place, and in order to do this, it was part of their policy to keep South Carolina as much out of sight as possible." The resolutions adopted by the meeting were drawn up by a former inhabitant of South Carolina and local leader of the Nullifiers in 1832. Because of the prejudice against South Carolina, these resolutions were not offered in convention and then referred to the proper committee according to customary procedure, but were sent informally and directly to the committee. Reported to the Convention, they were adopted without a general knowledge as to their authorship. It was charged that Wallace attended the Convention as the secret agent either of Calhoun or of South Carolina, sent to influence its action. Because of this suspicion he did not address

[8] Elmore to Seabrook, May 30, 1849, "Now as to Memminger and Kentucky—My opinion is Yes—Now if you plan to put me in requisition do it by putting us jointly in the commission." *Ibid.*

[9] A. Hutchinson to Calhoun, Oct. 5, 1849, *Calhoun Correspondence,* 1206.

the Convention as had been planned, but he did accept a seat on the floor of the Convention. He was forced to use caution in securing interviews with the Mississippi leaders and some circumspection in his conversations with them. With a view to finding out the nature of public sentiment in Mississippi and what measure of cooperation South Carolina could expect from the state, he conversed with Senator Jefferson Davis, Governor Matthews whose term of office was soon to expire, General John A. Quitman, then the Democratic candidate for governor and subsequently elected, Chief Justice Sharkey, leader of the Whigs, and others. As a result, though he got no definte promises, he could report to Governor Seabrook that Mississippi was fully aroused and would be in line with South Carolina when the hour of struggle should come. [10]

The action of the Convention was sufficient to warrant the opinion expressed by Wallace. Its resolutions took strong ground against the abolition of slavery in the District of Columbia, the prohibition of the inter-state slave trade, and the Wilmot Proviso, and recommended legislative provision for the calling of a state convention should any of the above measures be enacted into law by Congress. More important, however, for Calhoun and South Carolina was the call it made for a convention of the slave-holding states to be held at Nashville on the first Monday in June, 1850, "to devise and adopt some mode of resistance" to Northern aggression. [11]

---

[10] Wallace to Seabrook, Oct. 20, 1849, indorsed, "report of Gen. Wallace, special agent to the state of Mississippi," and Nov. 7, 1849, indorsed, "From Gen. D. Wallace in relation to his mission to Mississippi," Seabrook MSS. In a letter dated June 4, 1850, printed in the Jackson *Southron*, Wallace denied the charge that he had attended the Convention as an agent of South Carolina or Calhoun to influence its deliberations. See A. C. Cole, "The South and the Rights of Secession in the Early Fifties," in *Miss. Valley Hist. Rev.*, I, 377, n.

[11] Hearon, *Miss. and the Comp. of 1850*, 63-68.

The South Carolina legislature was the first in the Southern states to meet after the Mississippi October convention. Governor Seabrook, in his annual message, spoke openly of the possibility of disunion should all efforts fail to check consolidation and federal aggression. He hailed with satisfaction the call for a Southern convention, the paramount object of which, he said, was to preserve the Union in conformity to the principles of the Constitution, and should that prove impossible then to protect "at all hazards, the freedom, sovereignty, and independence of the members which compose it." He suggested that the governor be empowered to call the legislature in special session, or to issue writs for a state convention in case the Wilmot Proviso or any similar measure should be enacted by Congress. To prepare the state for any emergency, he urged the creation of a new division of militia fully armed and equipped for actual service, and appropriations of $50,000 for the purchase of arms and ammunition and of $30,000 as a contingent fund subject to the draft of the governor. [12]

On the evening of December 7 the members of the legislature met in legislative caucus, and hence unofficially, to consider the Mississippi call for a Southern convention. The caucus endorsed the movement and expressed its confidence that the people of South Carolina would support any measure which the convention might propose. It recommended that the people of the state meet in their respective parishes and districts the following April to elect delegates who should meet at some convenient point in each Congressional district and there choose from each of such districts two delegates to represent South Carolina at Nashville. Three days later the caucus chose as delegates at large to the Southern Convention, Langdon Cheves, Franklin H.

[12] Message of the Governor, Nov. 27, 1849, *S. C. Senate Journal*, 1849, 10-28.

Elmore, Robert W. Barnwell, and James H. Hammond. [13]
Cheves was the former president of the Second Bank of the
United States. He was a planter, long retired from public life,
and had recently refused a seat in the United States Senate. In
1832 he had opposed nullification and advocated a Southern convention as the proper means of securing redress and at the same
time preventing violence and disunion. In 1844, when Rhett
was leading a movement for separate state action against the
tariff, Cheves wrote a lengthy and fiery letter on disunion to the
editor of the *Mercury*. In this he admitted that the tariff was
oppressive, but abolition, he declared, was the great issue that
the South would have to meet, and to meet it the South should
not fear to face disunion. Separate state action he opposed,
and urged South Carolina to work for action in cooperation with
other Southern states. [14] Elmore, a former member of Congress,
was president of the Bank of the State of South Carolina. [15]
Barnwell was formerly president of South Carolina College. [16]
Hammond was a planter, who since the expiration of his term as
governor of the state had not engaged actively in politics. In
1832, as a nullifier he had aided in the preparations for armed
resistance to federal authority, and twelve years later when governor of the state he had urged opposition to the tariff and
abolition, by physical force if necessary. But in 1848 he doubted
the constitutionality of nullification. [17]

In regular session the South Carolina legislature refused
to sanction the military measures proposed by Governor Sea-

[13] Columbia *Tri-Weekly South Carolinian*, Dec. 8, 11, 1849.
[14] C. S. Boucher, *The Nullification Controversy in South Carolina*, 199-
200; *Mercury*, Sept. 11, 1844; J. B. O'Neall, *Bench and Bar in South Carolina*, I, 137.
[15] O'Neall, *Bench and Bar*, II, 95-96.
[16] National Cyclopaedia of America Biography, XI, 32.
[17] Boucher, *Nullification in S. C.*, 249, 269, 276, 279; *S. C. Senate
Journal*, 1844, 17-20; Hammond to Simms, Jan. 14, 1848, Hammond MSS.

brook and appropriated only $7,500 for the purchase of arms. [18]
It did accept the other proposal made by the governor to the
extent of providing ''in the event of the passage by Congress of
the Wilmot Proviso, or any kindred measure, that his Excellency
the Governor be requested forthwith to convene the legislature,
in order to take such steps as the rights, interest and honor ot
this State, and of the whole South, shall demand.'' [19] It furthermore adopted a resolution of full response to the sentiments of
the South Carolina delegation in Congress as expressed by one
of them, ''that if slavery be abolished in the District of Columbia by Congress, or the Wilmot Proviso be adopted, the Union
will be dissolved.'' [20]

The action of the South Carolina legislature on the call for
a Southern convention was in complete accord with the prevailing sentiments of all factions within the state. It signified a
willingness, which had long existed, for the participation by
South Carolina in cooperative measures for the defense of
Southern rights, and it provided for that cooperation by means
of delegates, unofficially chosen by the legislature and by the
people in their primary assemblies. Beyond this it wisely did
not go. It did not attempt to dictate or even give expression to
its views as to the proper action that should be taken by the
Nashville Convention. For the time being the state-actionists
were silent, for united Southern resistance seemed probable and
state action had been advocated by them chiefly because they had
believed any other mode of resistance impossible. Open opposition to the proposed convention 'here was none. There was
throughout the state a noticeable dimunition of agitation as
compared with the corresponding months of the two preceding
years. During the time intervening between the appointment of

[18] S. C. Reports and Resolutions, 1849, 310.
[19] Ibid., 313, 314.
[20] Ibid., 414.

the Central Committee of Vigilance and Safety in May and the Mississippi Convention of October, there was an almost complete silence on the well worn topics of Northern aggression and Southern resistance. Following the call issued from Mississippi there was some discussion of a Southern convention but little of the violent agitation of preceding years. There was no need to agitate in South Carolina in favor of the Southern Convention, and violent opposition to Clay's proposed compromise did not develop until late in the spring of 1850.

The purpose of the Nashville Convention and the action it should take were variously viewed. In the Columbia *South Carolinian* the proposal was made that the Convention nominate Calhoun for the presidency. Such lack of understanding drew forth immediate protests from other papers in the state and earned a well merited rebuke from Calhoun.[21] The conservative Charleston *Courier*, which for the most part had maintained a dignified silence and had always spoken with moderation on the issues about which most other South Carolina papers raved, came out in hearty support of the Nashville Convention. The object of this Convention, it thought, should be to voice "the united resolve of the South no longer to submit to aggression, outrage and insult, but on the contrary, to uphold her institutions, her rights and her sacred honor, 'peaceably if she can, forcibly if she must.'" The result of such a demand would be a "peaceful acquiescence in the rightful demands of the united South—or a peaceful separation of a family, in which there is an end of concord."[22] For once the *Mercury* spoke wisely and moderately. It saw no need to go beyond the resolutions of

[21] *Mercury*, Nov. 14, 15, 1849; *Courier*, Nov. 15, 1849; *Spartan*, Nov. 22, 1849; Calhoun to editor of *Carolinian*, Nov. 16, 1849, in *Tri-Weekly South Carolinian*, May 25, 1850; Calhoun to Hammond, Dec. 7, 1849, *Calhoun Correspondence*, 776.

[22] *Courier*, Oct. 31, Nov. 7, 15, 30, 1849.

Mississippi; South Carolina was willing and waiting for Southern defense of honor and interest; it was better that she cheer-
fully accept the leadership of others in the common cause rather
than by further advance endanger the success of the Southern
Movement. [23]

There were some papers in the state, however, not so prudent as the *Mercury* nor so moderate in opinion as the *Courier*.
These could not restrain their hatred of the Union. One editor
quite frankly admitted this sentiment: ''Let us not reluctantly
choose between the alternatives presented, of union, infamy and
ruin on the one hand, or disunion on the other. Give us the latter; the sooner the better.'' And again, ''We hold it to be the
sacred duty of the South, enjoined by every sentiment of pa-
triotism, honor and interest, to demand a dissolution of the
Union.'' [24] Another inspired his readers with these sentiments:
''To us of the South, the Union as it is, is a curse and not a bless-
ing. It is made an engine of oppression . . . We have
every faith that the South will either have their rights under
the Constitution or dissolve the Union.'' [25]

During March and April public meetings of citizens were
held in the districts and parishes at which delegates were chosen,
in accordance with the advice of the members of the legislature,
to attend the conventions in each congressional district by which
the delegates to Nashville should be selected. The resolutions of
these primary meetings, representing the opinions of those interested enough to participate, were not violent in tone, nor did
they attempt to dictate the action that the Nashville Convention
should take. But they did declare the opinion that either their
rights as they understood them should be protected and guaranteed or a dissolution of the Union ought to be effected. In so

[23] *Mercury*, Nov. 14, 15, Dec. 1, 1849.
[24] *Spartan*, Jan. 24, Feb. 21, 1850.
[25] *Winyah Observer*, Jan. 19, 1850.

far as the terms, ''dissolution of the Union'' and ''disunion''
were more openly used instead of the vaguer ''resistance at all
hazards and to the last extremity,'' these meetings represent an
advance over the previous position assumed by the people of the
state. Yet even at times when ''disunion'' was frankly spoken
of as the alternative to ''submission'' there was also expressed
a desire and a hope that a settlement of the whole question at
issue between the sections might be made whereby the rights of
the South would be guaranteed, the Constitution maintained,
and the Union preserved. On the other hand there was occa-
sionally expressed the extreme opinion that nothing but an entire
separation from that section which had ''trampled under foot
the rights of the South'' could afford a remedy for the grievances of the slaveholding states. [26]

The meetings of delegates in the various congressional districts, held May 6, 1850, contented themselves with the election
of delegates to Nashville and refrained from adopting the customary reports and resolutions. Of these delegates the most
prominent were: R. Barnwell Rhett, F. W. Pickens, Civil War
governor, R. F. W. Allston, Governor of South Carolina, 1856-
58, James Chesnut, United States senator in 1860, and D. F.
Jamison, president of the secession convention of 1860. [27]

Calhoun lost no opportunity, he wrote James H. Hammond,
''to give the great cause an impulse.'' He urged upon his cor-
respondents in various states the necessity of backing what he
termed ''the Mississippi movement,'' and of sending delegates to
the Nashville Convention. It was a subject uppermost in his
mind and its failure to meet he would have considered a great, if
not a fatal, misfortune. By January he felt assured that the

[26] *Mercury*, Mar. 21, 27, Apr. 13, 16, 18, 29, 1850; *Spartan*, Mar. 14;
Tri-Weekly South Carolinian, Mar. 5, 1850; *Winyah Observer*, Apr. 10,
1850.

[27] List of delegates in *Mercury*, May 11, 1850; *Spartan*, May 16, 1850.

convention would meet. [28] For a time it seemed that Calhoun's hope for a united South on the slavery question was about to be fulfilled. Following the call issued by the Mississippi October Convention and the response thereto by the members of the South Carolina legislature, in Virginia, Georgia, Florida, Alabama, Mississippi, Texas and Arkansas, the legislatures endorsed the movement and provided for the election of delegates. In addition, the legislatures of Georgia, Alabama, Mississippi and Virginia provided for the calling of state conventions in case Congress should pass the Wilmot Proviso or other measures deemed hostile to the interests of slavery. [29]

It has been charged against Calhoun that he was desirous of destroying the Union. His real desire was to preserve the Union, if at the same time he could preserve what he considered to be the rights of the South. He was undeniably first a citizen of the South and only secondly a citizen of the United States. His correspondence gives constant proof of this. On December 27, 1846, he wrote to his daughter, "I desire above all things to save the whole; but if that cannot be, to save the portion where Providence has cast my lot, at all events." He believed that unless the North became convinced that the South was in earnest and put an end to the attacks upon Southern institutions, the time would come when nothing could save the South but a dissolution of the Union. He desired a Southern convention to give expression to these ideas, and to force upon the North the conviction that the Union was in danger and would be dissolved unless the demands of the South with regards to the slavery controversy were acceded to.

[28] Calhoun to A. P. Calhoun, Oct. 22, 1849; to Herschel V. Johnson, Nov. 1, 1849; to Hammond, Dec. 7, 1849, Jan. 4, 1850, *Calhoun Correspondence*, 772, 773, 775, 778.

[29] H. V. Ames, "Calhoun and the Secession Movement," in *Old Penn*, XVI, 247; D. T. Herndon, "The Nashville Convention of 1850", in *Pub. of Ala. Hist. Soc., Transactions*, V, 213-216.

In the summer of 1849 he still thought that the Union might be preserved, though he feared that perhaps the process of sectionalization had gone too far for any hope of a continuance of the political connection between North and South. In August of that year he wrote to Senator Foote of Mississippi: ''In considering it [a Southern Convention], I assume that the first desire of every true-hearted Southern man is, to save, if possible, the Union, as well as ourselves; but if both cannot be, then to save ourselves at all events. Such is my determination, as far as it lies in my power. Fortunately for us, the road which leads to both, yet lies in the same direction. We have not reached the fork yet, if we are ever to do it. Without concert of action on the part of the South, neither can be saved; by it, if it be not too long delayed, it is possible both yet may be.'' [30]

Early in 1850 Calhoun seems to have become convinced that a permanent settlement of the whole slavery question such as he considered essential for a continuance of the slaveholding states in the Union could not be made. [31] He hoped that the debate in Congress would convince the South that it could not with safety remain in the Union as things then stood and that there was little or no prospect of any change for the better. [32] Compromise, any settlement short of his terms, was unacceptable to him. The Wilmot Proviso he had opposed only as one phase of the whole slavery controversy. It had raised the issue between the sections, but to Calhoun's mind the territorial aspect of the question was only one and not perhaps the most important aspect of the whole question of slavery. He had used the Wilmot Proviso to arouse the South, but in the Southern Address he had sought to broaden the basis for the Southern movement by including in

[30] Calhoun to Foote, Aug. 3, 1849, *Mercury*, June 4, 1851.

[31] Calhoun to Mrs. T. G. Clemson, Feb. 24, 1850, *Calhoun Correspondence*, 783.

[32] Calhoun to Hammond, Feb. 16, 1850, *ibid.*, 781.

that manifesto of Southern grievances every evidence he could find of hostility to and aggressions upon slavery. He had been convinced for more than twenty years that the institution of slavery was in danger and that the South, rather than merely to repel attacks, should force the issue. Let the outposts of slavery be carried and the institution would be doomed. In 1850 the time for action had come; to force the issue was the idea constantly in his mind. Nothing short of a permanent settlement of the question within the Union or a dissolution of the Union was his desire.

"Nothing short of the terms I propose, can settle it finally and permanently," he wrote just three weeks before his death. "Indeed, it is difficult to see how two peoples so different and hostile can exist together in one Unon." [33] The terms Calhoun proposed were given to the country in his famous speech of the fourth of March. [34] Too weak to deliver it himself, it was read to the Senate by his friend Senator Mason of Virgina. In this carefully written exposition of his views Calhoun stressed the all important fact, to him, that the equilibrium between the two sections had been destroyed; that consequently all branches of the government were in the control of the North; and that as a result, in all questions of vital interest between the sections, the South would be sacrificed. To Calhoun, of course, the North was the free states, the South, the slave states. Slavery, which the people of the South felt bound "by every consideration of interest and safety to defend," was the vital question. He declared that the ultimate aim of the anti-slavery movement in the North was the total abolition of the institution of slavery in all the states, and that unless some decisive measures were taken to

[33] Calhoun to T. G. Clemson, Mar. 10, 1850, *Calhoun Correspondence*, 784. On the general question of Calhoun's opinions and purposes in the last year of his life, see *ibid.*, 763-783, *passim*.

[34] Calhoun, *Works*, IV, 542-573.

prevent this, unless a full and final settlement were made; the South would be forced ''to choose between abolition and secession.'' The terms of this final settlement Calhoun stated: equal rights in the territories, faithful fulfillment of the stipulations relative to fugitive slaves, cessation of anti-slavery agitation, and a constitutional amendment restoring to the South the power of protecting herself that she had possessed before the destruction of the equilibrium between the sections. The exact nature of his proposed amendment Calhoun did not here disclose, but a posthumous work explains in general his idea that the end he sought might be effected by the creation of a dual executive, its members representing the respective sections and each possessed of the veto power over all legislation.[35]   Calhoun closed his speech with an appeal for a frank avowal on both sides of what was intended to be done towards a settlement of the questions at issue. To the senators from the North he addressed himself: ''If you, who represent the stronger portion, cannot agree to settle them on the broad principle of justice and duty, say so; and let the states we both represent agree to separate and part in peace. If you are unwilling we should part in peace, tell us so, and we shall know what to do, when you reduce the question to submission or resistance.''

This was Calhoun's last important speech in the Senate. He had spoken frankly and presented to the Senate and the country his alternative to a dissolution of the Union, and it was probably his hope that it would similarly be presented by the Southern Convention. He stated frequently enough in his correspondence his desire that the Southern Convention present the alternative of justice to the South, as he conceived it, or a dissolution of the Union, but whether on the exact terms as outlined in his final speech it is impossible to say. He was extreme-

[35] ''A Discourse on the Constitution and Government of the United States'', in Calhoun, *Works*, I, 111-406, see pp. 391-392.

ly anxious that some of the delegates to that convention visit Washington on their way to Nashville and consult there with members from the South. [36] Shortly before his death he began to dictate a series of resolutions, evidently intended for this convention, which were never completed. They were directed against the exclusion of slavery from the territories and the admission of California into the Union; and the final resolution of the uncompleted draft reads: "Resolved that the time has arrived when the said States [i. e., "the States composing the Southern portion of th Union"] owe it to themselves and the other States comprising the Union to settle fully and forever all the questions at issue between them." [37] This was Calhoun's final and well matured opinion. A few days later, on March 31, he died, leaving South Carolina without a leader strong enough to prevent the bitter internal struggle into which she was destined soon to fall.

The attitude of Calhoun represented probably that of the majority of those in his state who had any opinions on the question of union and disunion. It may be true, as Judge Beverly Tucker of Virginia wrote to James H. Hammond, that Calhoun, instead of being the moving cause of excitement in South Carolina, as many thought, restrained it and restrained himself. [38]

[36] Calhoun to Hammond, Feb. 16, 1850, *Calhoun Correspondence*, 781.

[37] *Calhoun Correspondence*, 785-787; Joseph A. Scoville, to whom Calhoun dictated the resolutions, did not know whether they were for the Senate or for Nashville. Scoville to Hammond, Apr. 18, 1850, Hammond MSS. Their wording is sufficient evidence that they were not intended for the Senate. A copy was sent to Hammond but they do not seem to have been used at Nashville.

[38] Calhoun "died nobly, and his last act redeems all the errors of his life......I have heard of those who rejoiced in his death as providential. I hope it may prove so, but not in the way intended by them. They considered him as the moving cause of excitement in South Carolina. You and I know that he restrained it and restrained himself. When he went home in March, '33, he was prepared to say all that he said in his last speech and much more had others been prepared to hear it. I know it from his own lips......" May 7, 1850, Hammond MSS.

But such restraint for the past ten years at least had been applied with a view to prevent assumption by the state of a position too far in advance of the other slaveholding states. The
position he assumed in his last speech in the Senate earned the
praise of those who had privately condemned him for his back-
wardness. Certainly there was but little difference in the position of a man who demanded impossible conditions for the preservation of the Union and those who believed that conditions
were such as to warrant the immediate withdrawal of the Southern states from the Union. Regarding the feeling in South Carolina at this time, a traveler reported to Judge Tucker that he
met within the State but one man not ripe for disunion and un-
prepared to reject any terms of compromise which should leave
the South, as Tucker said, ''without excuse for the great step
on which our best interests depend.'' [39]   The one exception to
this sweeping and perhaps hopefully exaggerated statement was
James Louis Petigru.

Since the days of Nullification the Unionists in South Carolina had constantly decreased in number until in 1850 there
were but a handful of men who were willing to preserve the
Union at almost any cost. Petigru was one of the most uncom-
promising of these. Joel R. Poinsett was another. The former
was a Whig, the latter a Democrat. The correspondence that
took place between Richard Yeadon, Unionist in 1832 and former editor of the Charleston *Courier,* and Poinsett, illustrates
fully the positions of those of the old Union party who remained
true to the Union and those who had reached the conclusion,
however unwillingly, that its dissolution might be necessary.

Yeadon wrote Poinsett on March 1, 1850 that the Charleston
leaders wished to send him as a delegate to Nashville, ''having
in view the preservation, if practicable, of our mighty and glor-

[39] *Ibid.*

ious union, but the assertion and maintenance, at all hazard and in any event, of the just rights and constitutional equality of the Southern States.'' Poinsett replied expressing a willingness to attend the Nashville Convention, ''provided its objects are 'limited to the preservation of our mighty and glorious union and the constitutional equality of the Southern states.' But,'' he continued, ''if 'their assertion and maintenance at all hazards and in any event' be meant to imply the dissolution of the Union of the United States, I feel constrained to declare that I never will by any act of mine sanction such an alternative.'' And when informed that a public avowal of such sentiments would make impossible his election as a delegate, he flatly refused to serve. In explanation he continued: ''I have been long aware that the district and state are prepared for the last extremity; and, as I conscientiously believe such a measure will lead to immediate civil war and too probably terminate in defeat and humiliation, it would be wrong in me to yield to the torrent of public opinion and by any act of mine aid in the perpetration of our own destruction. . . . If the revolution comes, for there can be no peaceable secession or dissolution of the union, I am ready to take my part and stand among the sons of the South in the ranks or in organizing our defenses but without hope.'' [40] A little later Poinsett refused to permit himself to be considered as a possible delegate from the fourth Con-

[40] Richard Yeadon to Joel R. Poinsett, Mar. 1, 1850; Poinsett to Yeadon, Mar. 6, 18, 1850. In a draft of his letter of Mar. 18, Poinsett wrote and then crossed out the following: ''I may be wrong but it appears to me that the same minds and the same views which governed them at the banquet which drew from the great man [Jackson] this celebrated sentiment [Our Union, it must be preserved] are again at work for evil. They are nearer the attainment of their object now than they were then; but they are the more near to their own destruction; for the revolution will surely overwhelm them in its mighty billows.'' Poinsett MSS. Jackson's famous toast was given at the Jefferson birthday dinner of the South Carolina group in Washington, Apr. 15, 1830. See J. S. Bassett, *Life of Andrew Jackson*, II, 554-555.

gressional district. Unable to sanction the alternative of dissolution in the last resort, which the people of Marion and Darlington had publicly avowed, he however made no public opposition
to the movement at this time, for he did not desire to weaken in
the slightest degree the effect of the demonstration on the part of
the South. [41] Nor did anyone in South Carolina now speak out
in opposition to the Nashville Convention and the dissolution
of the Union which was expected to follow it.

The effect upon old Union men of anti-slavery agitation is
illustrated by the position that Yeadon took. "Ardent as has
been and still is my devotion to the Union—," he wrote, "deeply
as I would deplore its dissolution as a dire calamity to our country,—South as well as North—and to mankind—yet am I convinced that the passage of the Wilmot Proviso, or any equiva-
lent hostile and unconstitutional action of Congress, on the question of slavery, would be a justifying cause of disunion, and impose it on the South as a duty and a necessity. If we submit to
such an aggression . . . we will but encourage our political and fanatic foes to put their feet on our necks and accomplish our destruction and our ruin." [42] Ex-governor David
Johnson, another old Unionist leader, likewise could not but de-
spair of the Union because of the war against slave owners. [43]

Of quite another type of opinion were those who may be
termed disunionists *per se,* men who had no wish to save the
Union, who not only would have welcomed disunion but who were
working hopefully for disunion and looking forward to a slaveholding Southern confederacy. One of these was James H.
Hammond, whom his friend William Gilmore Simms hoped to
see succeed Calhoun in the Senate and help "bring on the catas-

[41] Poinsett to E. Waterman, Mar. 30, 1850, Poinsett MSS.
[42] Yeadon to Poinsett, Mar. 9, 1850, Poinsett MSS.
[43] David Johnson to J. S. Sims, May 6, 1850, *Spartan,* May 30, 1850.

trophe.''[44] From Virginia Judge Tucker urged that South Carolina should secede and form the nucleus of a new Confederacy, and proposed to Hammond that the Nashville Convention be used to demand impossible conditions for a continuance of the Union and thus force the withdrawal of the Southern states.[45] The proposal of J. M. Walker, Charleston lawyer, former member of the state legislature, and non-slaveowner, was that the Nashville Convention ''should assume at once legislative authority and under the same responsibilities as rested upon the first Congress, declare independence.''[46]

Hammond thought that the Union always had been and always would be a disadvantage to the South and that the sooner the South got rid of it the better. He feared abolition and the reduction of the South to the condition of Hayti, should she remain in the Union save as the equal of the North, and this equality he did not believe it possible to obtain. The formation of a Southern confederacy he thought desirable and ultimately inevitable, and he saw in the abolitionists the instruments of God working towards this purpose. He saw in the North and in the South two distinct ''Social Compacts'' and believed that inevitably they must separate. He believed that the time for separation had come but he thought that the Nashville Convention, being a non-official body, should take little action beyond calling a ''General Congress of the South.'' His chief fear was that before action could be taken the North would give way and promise enough temporarily to appease the South and defer disunion.[47]

[44] Simms to Hammond, (Apr.) 1850, Hammond MSS.
[45] Tucker to Hammond, Dec. 27, 1849, Feb. 8, 1850, *ibid.*
[46] J. M. Walker to Hammond, Feb. 25, 1850, *ibid.*
[47] J. H. Hammond to Calhoun, Feb. 19, 1849, Mar. 5, 1850, *Calhoun Correspondence*, 1193-94, 1210-12; J. H. Hammond to Major Hammond, Feb. 1, 1850, to Lewis Tappan, July 9, 1850, to W. H. Trescott, Aug. 25, 1850, Hammond MSS.

Such was the feeling in South Carolina just prior to the meeting of the Nashville Convention. In other Southern states the introduction of Clay's compromise plan and the prospect of some adjustment of the questions at issue without the enactment of the Wilmot Proviso somewhat lessened the disunion sentiment. Especially was this true with the Whigs. But the proposed compromise was almost unanimously condemned in South Carolina. A meeting of the citizens of Charleston unanimously declared that the measures reported in the United States Senate "purporting to be a *Compromise*" ought not to receive the sanction and support of the South, and condemned individually each provision of that report. Some other public meetings took similar action. Most of the newspapers, the *Courier* excepted and therefore denounced by the others, found nothing in the proposed compromise that could afford any satisfaction to the South. Some demanded the extension of the Missouri Compromise line as the only acceptable settlement, while others declared that no compromise would be respected by the North, and demanded disunion as the only final settlement. Specifically each of the five propositions included in Clay's plan met with opposition. The admission of California as a free state, with her "illegally" organized constitution, was termed a practical enforcement of the Wilmot Proviso "in a more odious and insulting form." A truer reason for opposition was given when it was pointed out that the admission of California would give to the free states two additional senators and two representatives. Calhoun in his last speech had declared that the admission of California was the test question, and would give proof whether the North was willing to grant equality to the South or proposed to overthrow completely the sectional balance of power. The plan for the territorial organization of New Mexico and Utah was found unsatisfactory because it did not guarantee the protection of slavery, and because the North would never admit those territories save

as free states. The settlement of the territorial disputes between
Texas and the United States was denounced as an abolitionist
scheme for making free soil and ultimately free states of territory in which slavery existed by Texan law. The abolition of
the slave trade was of course declared an unconstitutional attack
on the outposts of slavery. Even the proposed new fugitive-
slave law was objected to because it permitted the escaped slave
a jury trial, and at best it would never be enforced. [48] Clearly
South Carolina did not desire to compromise.

Shortly before the Nashville Convention met, two members
of Congress from South Carolina publicly advised their constituents as to the situation in Washington and gave their personal
views on the proposed compromise. Representative Burt, who
had long since despaired of securing even the Missouri Compromise line, reported that there was no hope of a satisfactory or
even any adjustment of the sectional issues, and declared his conviction that Northern hostility to slavery was more ferocious,
more universal, more confident of its strength, and more assured
of its victim than ever before. [49] General Wallace denounced the
Clay compromise measures, dwelt at length upon the social and
political equality of the two races that would result from abolition, and declared that the people of the South had nothing to
hope from the government of the United States. [50]

The Nashville Convention met June 3, 1850, and elected

[48] Charleston Meeting, *Mercury*, May 21, 1850; Meeting in Union, June
3, *Spartan*, June 13, 1850; *South Carolinian*, May 14, 16, June 1, 1850;
Spartan, May 23, 1850; *Winyah Observer*, June 19, 1850; *Mercury*, May
20, 21, 22, 23, 24, 1850.

[49] A. Burt to F. W. Pickens and Drayton Nance, delegates to Nashville,
in *Mercury*, May 28, 1850.

[50] D. Wallace to the People of the 1st Congressional district of South
Carolina, *ibid.*, June 5, 1850, *Sparatn*, June 20, 1850.

Judge William L. Sharkey, of Mississippi, president.[51] Delegates from nine states were present, Virginia, South Carolina, Georgia, Florida, Alabama, Mississippi, Texas, Arkansas, and Tennessee. In the South Carolina delegation of eighteen there was only one vacancy. Elmore, appointed to Calhoun's place in the Senate, had died late in May. More advanced in sentiment than the other delegations, that of South Carolina did not take a very prominent part in the proceedings on the floor of the convention. An exception to this was the speech by Pickens, ending with this sentiment, "Equality now! Equality forever! or Independence." Rhett wrote the address of the convention to the Southern states, and Hammond, with some difficulty, got it through the committee and adopted by the convention. The address reviewed at length the aggressions of the North and the growing hostility to slavery, and declared that the position of the South in the Union was growing from bad to worse. It condemned the compromise measure then before Congress, but it expressed a willingness on the part of the South to accept an extension of the Missouri Compromise line. A long series of resolutions adopted by the convention set forth the familiar doctrine of the equal rights of the states in the territories and the newer doctrine of the duty of the Congress to protect those rights, but proposed "as an extreme concession" a division of the territory between the sections along the line of 36° 30'. The final resolution declared that the convention did not "feel at liberty to discuss the methods suitable for a resistance to measures not yet adopted." But it was agreed that in the event of the failure of Congress to meet the demands of the convention, it should meet

[51] The most complete account of the Nashville Convention is Herndon, "The Nashville Convention of 1850", in *Ala. Hist. Soc. Transactions*, V, 203-237. See also St. George L. Sioussat, "Tennessee, the Compromise of 1850, and the Nashville Convention", in *Miss. Valley Hist. Rev.*, II, 311-347; and F. Newberry, "The Nashville Convention and Southern Sentiment of 1850", in *So. Atl. Quarterly*, XI, 259-273.

again after the adjournment of Congress.　On June 12, 1850, the first session of the Nashville Convention came to a close. [52] In the opinion of Hammond, its results did not amount to much save that it would strengthen the hands of the South in Congress. "The great point," he wrote, "is that the South *has met,* has acted with great harmony in a nine days' convention, and above all *has agreed to meet again."* [53]

[52] Pamphlet: "Resolutions and Address adopted by the Southern Convention held at Nashville......"; *Mercury,* June 11, 12, 1850; Ames, *State Documents,* 263-269.

[53] Hammond to Simms, June 16, 1850, Hammond MSS.

CHAPTER IV

The Compromise Rejected

The work of the Nashville Convention was not such as to arouse any great degree of enthusiasm in the hearts of the disunionists. In South Carolina its recommendations of a division of the territories between the sections by the line of 36° 30′ was magnified into an "Ultimatum of the South."[1] Fourth of July toasts offered throughout the state were violent in tone and frankly in favor of disunion, should Congress pay no heed to the recommendations of the Convention. One may illustrate: "Bring what it will, Revolution or Disunion, still we say, 36 30 and nothing less."[2] The newspapers accepted the work of the convention, though the more radical of them did so with no great enthusiasm. The *Mercury* thought that the proceedings at Nashville received the entire approbation and the zealous support of the people of Charleston, but it took pains to declare that any settlement short of the Missouri Compromise line would "blow up the confederacy."[3] The *Spartan* rather reluctantly supported the proposal as an extreme concession by the South, and as affording, if accepted, a temporary respite from assaults; but it believed an ultimate separation of the sections both desirable and inevitable.[4] Public meetings heard from the members of the South Carolina delegation and declared the Missouri Compromise line the utmost concession that the South would make.

[1] *South Carolinian,* June 18, 1850.

[2] This sentiment offered at Beaufort. Proceedings of the meeting in *Mercury,* July 12, 1850.

[3] June 21, 22, 1850.

[4] July 11, 1850.

Rhett had hardly returned from Nashville before he began
a series of fiery speeches in advocacy of a dissolution of the
Union. At Charleston, on June 21, he declared that the Nashville Convention had proffered settlements which the North
would not accept, and on which the South would not yield. ˙ He
prophesied that the Nashville Convention would rank as one of
those great events which mark the beginning of mighty changes.
"We are in the beginning of a revolution!" he exclaimed. After dwelling at length upon the disadvantages of the Union to
the South, he pictured the prosperity and the advantages to
trade and commerce that would follow the free-trade policy of
an independent South.   And true to his previous tendencies
towards separate state action, Rhett declared that should all
other states desert her, South Carolina would struggle alone for
liberty and independence. [5]   In the following month, on July 24,
Rhett spoke in St. Helena Parish on the probable and possible
destinies of a Southern confederacy.   "Treason" had taken
strong root in this section, the reporter wrote, and Rhett's sentiments were received with approbation. [6] In August, Rhett and
Yancey were preaching disunion in Georgia. [7]   Early in September Rhett was again in South Carolina and on the fourth day
of that month addressed six hundred citizens of St. Bartholomew's Parish. He recited the usual Southern rights and Southern wrongs; he urged a Southern confederacy; he scouted the
idea of war with the North, and predicted that soon Northern
men would be seeking admission into the new union. The following enlightening account of a part of Rhett's speech was thus
reported:

"Speaking of the possibility of the emancipation of slavery,

[5] Speech of R. B. Rhett, June 21, *Mercury*, July 20, 1850.
[6] *Palmetto Post*, quoted in *Mercury*, Aug. 16, 1850.
[7] James A. Meriwether to Howell Cobb, Aug. 24, 1850, *Toombs, Stephens, and Cobb Correspondence*, 210.

he very happily showed to non-slaveholders here, what their condition would be in such an event. It would terminate in amalga-
mation or extermination......Shall the African rule here? No!
We will not be governed by the African; neither will we be by
the Yankees! We must secede. Georgia will lead off, South
Carolina will go with her, Alabama will soon follow, and Mississippi will not be long behind her......Within eighteen months
we will have the whole South with us, and more than that; we
will extend our borders, we will have New Mexico, Utah, and
California. Utah already has slaves. We will march into California, and we will ask them if they will have slaves, and her
people will answer, Ay, we will have slaves. And what of Mexico? Why, when we are ready for them, and her people are
fitted to come among us, we will take her too, or as much of her
as we want.'' [8]

F. W. Pickens expressed a view similar to Rhett's regarding
the work of the Nashville Convention. Comparing the condition
of the South with that of the colonies before the Revolution, he
said that the Southern states would have to move step by step,
and he pictured the Nashville Convention as the first step
towards equality or independence. [9] Hammond agreed with the
sentiments expressed by Rhett in his Charleston speech, but he
regretted the fact that they had been uttered. He had worked
at Nashville to overcome the prejudice against South Carolina
and to secure a second meeting of the convention. He expected
the struggle throughout the South against submission to be both
difficult and long unless the North by increasing aggressions
should aid the disunionists, and he feared that Rhett's words, es-

---

[8] This speech, not written out in full, is reported in the *Mercury*, Sept.
12, 1850. Some corrections were made by Rhett in *ibid.*, Sept. 13, 1850.
The quotation here given, then, represents correctly Rhett's ideas, though
not his exact words.

[9] Speech near Glenn Springs, Aug. 10, in *Spartan*, Aug. 22, 1850.

pecially his reference to the Nashville Convention as a revolutionary step,.would be used by submissionists against South Carolina and the resistance movement. "Such men spoil all movements," he wrote in disgust. [10]

In the meantime, Congress had paid little attention to the so-called ultimatum of the Nashville Convention. The death of Taylor and the succession of Fillmore to the presidency, with Webster as his Secretary of State, insured the success of Clay's plan of adjustment. On July 31, the bill for the territorial organization of Utah without the prohibition of slavery passed the Senate. Within the course of the next two months five separate bills, containing substantially Clay's proposals, were accepted by both houses. On September 20, the last of these, providing for the suppression of the slave trade in the District of Columbia, became a law. In the House the South Carolina delegation supported only the fugitive-slave bill.

The time had now come to test the sincerity of those who had pledged resistance to the Wilmot Proviso, to the admission of California with her constitution prohibiting slavery, and to the prohibition of the slave trade in the District of Columbia. Moderate men, among them most of the Southern Whigs, who had been willing to resist the Wilmot Proviso, accepted the compromise. The radicals declared that the admission of California was worse than the proviso, and demanded resistance to the compromise. But in only four states, South Carolina, Georgia, Alabama, and Mississippi, was any serious movements in this direction begun.

The passage of the compromise measures served only to increase the disunion movement in South Carolina and to bring it more into the open. Where disunion had been deemed an alternative, it was now demanded as the only course left for the

[10] Hammond to Simms, June 27, to H. W. Conner, July 17, 1850, Hammond MSS.

South. Even the Charleston *Courier* considered the argument
exhausted and the time for action at hand, and was convinced
that a dissolution of the Union was inevitable.[11]   The *Mercury*
said, "No earthly power can save this Confederacy from dissolution."[12]   Its columns were filled with demands for disunion
and the formation of a Southern confederacy. The compromise
measures were denounced as giving nothing to the South and
everything to the North. It was declared that the fugitive slave
law would not be enforced or would soon be repealed.[13]

But the demand for a dissolution of the Union and the for·
mation of a Southern confederacy was not based so much on the
grounds of the injustice and unconstitutionality of the recent
acts of Congress *per se,* as on the conviction repeatedly asserted
that the institution of slavery was endangered by a continuance
of the Southern states within the Union. The editor of the
Spartan wrote: "The signs of the times disclose the solemn truth
that we must give up the Union or give up slavery."[14]   Another
editor stated the same opinion in other words when he declared
that "the question is *not* Union or disunion; but simply the ultimate abolition of slavery in the Union or its retention and
Southern independence out of it."[15]   A third, in one of the
great rice-planting sections of the state, argued that "the true
issue before us, is whether we will give up a Union oppressive
and hostile to us, or give up slavery which is indispensibly necessary to our very existence."[16]   Pamphleteers stressed the same
idea and urged a Southern confederacy as the remedy. One
argued that the North with the aid of new free states to be

[11] Nov. 7, 1850.
[12] Oct. 21, 1850.
[13] *Mercury,* Oct. 23, Nov. 7, 1850; *Spartan,* Oct. 31, 1850; *Winyah Ob
server,* Nov. 20, 1850.
[14] *Spartan,* Nov. 14, 1850.
[15] *Tri-Weekly South Carolinian,* Sept. 28, 1850.
[16] *Winyah Observer,* Dec. 14, 1850.

created out of the territories, would soon abolish slavery in the South. The result would be political and social equality for black and white, the loss of $15,000,000,000 capital and an equal loss in land depreciation, the abandonment of the cultivation of Southern staples and consequently poverty, distress, and ruin. As an alternative he pictured a prosperous and happy "Southern United States of America." [17] Another summarized his whole pamphlet of one hundred and fifty-two pages with these sentences: "There is Union and Abolition on one hand, and Disunion and Slavery on the other. Which of the two shall we choose?......Give us *SLAVERY* or *give us death.*" [18]

Upon the passage of the compromise measures South Carolina leaders looked to other Southern states for the beginning of resistance. Though urged to do so, Governor Seabrook decided not to call a special session of the legislature, preferring to await the movement of Georgia and one or two other states before committing South Carolina. But he was prepared, when the time should come, "to recommend the strongest measure that has been conceived." [19] On September 20, Seabrook sent letters, in identical terms, to the governors of Virginia, Alabama, and Mississippi informing them that the governor of Georgia would soon call a state convention, and asking whether their respective states were prepared to adopt any scheme to second Georgia "in her noble effort to preserve unimpaired the Union of '87." He assured them that as soon as the governors of two or more states

[17] (John Townsend) "The Southern States, Their Present Peril, and Their Certain Remedy......"

[18] Edward B. Bryan, "The Rightful Remedy. Addressed to the Slaveholders of the South."

[19] Seabrook to Col. J. A. Leland, Sept. 18, 21, 1850, Seabrook MSS. That of Sept. 21, printed in *Mercury*, Sept. 27, 1850. See I. W. Hayne to Hammond, Oct. 6, 1850, "I think we should give them (Ga., Ala., Miss.) time to come up to us before we proceed to extremities." Hammond MSS.

should assemble their legislatures or furnish some other evidence on the part of their states "of determined resistance, in disregard of consequences," he would call the South Carolina legislature with a view to the adoption of measures that, so far as it concerned his state, would "effectually arrest the career of an interested and despotic majority." [20]   This letter shows that Seabrook had already received information from Governor Towns of Georgia of his intention to call a state convention as recommended by legislative resolutions of the preceding February. [21]

Seabrook's reason for not calling the South Carolina legislature is indicated by the letter Towns wrote him on September 25. The situation in Georgia, he wrote, was critical, and though the people were prepared to act decisively, their leaders opposed the resistance measures that he desired. The resistance party had no strength to lose by any premature movement in any of the other states, and he feared that should South Carolina take any decided step it would contribute largely to the overthrow of the "true Southern party" in Georgia and the election of a submission majority to the state convention. He suggested that South Carolina make no move until the results of the election should be known. [22]

In Alabama Governor Collier, though urged to do so, did not think it wise to convene the legislature in special session. Yancey, however, led a movement for the organization of Southern Rights Associations throughout the state, and made the right of secession the issue in the campaign of the following

[20] Endorsed, ''Confidential letter to the Governors of Alabama, Virginia, and Mississippi, Sept. 20, '50.'' Seabrook MSS. Also printed in J. F. H. Claiborne, *Life and Correspondence of John A. Quitman*, II, 36.

[21] For these resolutions see *Ga. Laws*, 1849-50, 405-410.

[22] Gov. Towns to Gov. Seabrook, Sept. 25, 1850, Seabrook MSS.

year. [23] In Virginia, the compromise was accepted without serious opposition. But from Mississippi Seabrook received a favorable reply to his letter. Governor Quitman wrote that upon the passage of the bill for the admission of California he had decided to call the legislature in special session, and had only delayed that call, to give strength to his position, until the passage of the bill abolishing the slave trade in the District of Columbia. His proclamation called the legislature to meet the eighteenth of November. He informed the governor of South Carolina that it was his desire that the legislature should provide for a state convention with full power to annul the federal compact and establish new relations with other states. He looked to secession, and he reported the people of Mississippi probably ready for resistance regardless of consequences. [24]

The news of the action taken by the governors of Mississippi and Georgia stimulated a demand from Charleston for an immediate convocation of the South Carolina legislature. This pressure Governor Seabrook resisted to the extent of getting up a meeting in Columbia which recommended to him not to call the legislature. He did, however, prepare a proclamation calling the legislature for November 18, the day on which the Mississippi legislature was to meet, and only about two weeks before the time for the regular annual meeting, with the idea of stimulating Mississippi, Alabama, Florida, and Virginia to their duty and conciliating Georgia. This proclamation he submitted to Governor Towns with a request for information as to whether or not it would operate against the resistance party in Georgia. [25] Evi-

[23] Hearon, *Mississippi and the Compromise of 1850*, 188-189; Du Bose, *Life of Yancey*, 251-252; G. F. Mellen, ''Henry W. Hilliard and William L. Yancey,'' in *Sewanee Review, XVII*, 32-50.

[24] Quitman to Seabrook, Sept. 29, 1850, Seabrook MSS. Printed in part in Claiborne, *Life of Quitman*, II, 37. Quitman's proclamation in *ibid.*, 43.

[25] Seabrook to Towns, Oct. 8, 1850, Seabrook MSS.

dently the reply from Towns was unfavorable, for it was not issued. The reasons for taking no definite action in South Carolina, the fear that the cause of resistance would perhaps receive a fatal blow should that state attempt to take the lead, Seabrook explained at length to the governor of Mississippi, but he took pains to reiterate the assurance that South Carolina was prepared to second Mississippi or any other state "in any and every effort to arrest the career of a corrupt and despotic majority. She is ready and anxious," he continued, "for an immediate separation from a Union whose aim is a prostration of our political edifice. May I hope that Mississippi will begin the patriotic work, and allow the Palmetto banner the privilege of a place in her ranks?" [26]

It was the desire of the South Carolina leaders, wrote Seabrook, that united action be taken by a "Southern Congress, with full authority on the part of the states represented to secede from the Union forthwith, or to submit to the supreme authorities of the country propositions for a new bargain between the states, by which equality among the members of the confederacy and the protection of Southern property shall, in future, be put beyond the possibility of hazard." The secession of the Southern states acting either through a Southern congress or individually on the recommendation of such a Congress, preferably in the former manner and therefore with a "government actually in operation," or the presentation of demands for new constitutional guarantees for slavery, perhaps Calhoun's suggestion, was then the end sought by the governor of South Carolina. The call for such a congress he hoped could be secured from the Nashville Convention at its second session, from the Georgia Convention, or from the Mississippi legislature. [27] Such also, in gen-

---

[26] Seabrook to Quitman, Oct. 23, 1850, Claiborne, *Life of Quitman*, II, 37-38.

[27] *Ibid.*

eral, was the hope that Robert W. Barnwell, who had been appointed to the seat in the Senate left vacant by the death of Elmore, had expressed immediately upon the passage of the compromise measures. "I should think it inexpedient for South Carolina to move alone in this matter," he wrote. "If by action any state will give assurance of sustaining her, I should be decidedly for South Carolina seceding, thus forcing a Congress of slaveholding states to assemble. But I should think first to take counsel together in Nashville." [28]

Although Judge Sharkey accepted the compromise measures and refused to issue the call for the reassembling of the Southern Convention, delegates from seven states met in Nashville, Nov. 11, 1850. Most of the moderate men refused to attend and the convention was in complete control of the radicals. Cheves for the South Carolina delegation submitted a resolution, "That a secession, by the joint action of the slaveholding states, is the only efficient remedy for the aggravated wrongs which they now endure, and the enormous events which threaten them in the future, from the usurped and now unrestricted power of the Federal Government." In a fiery speech of three hours in length, he elaborated the idea of this resolution; he denounced and ridiculed "the glorious Union;" he pleaded for a union of the South and the establishment of a Southern confederacy. The Convention adopted resolutions affirming the right of secession, denouncing the compromise measures, and, as Barnwell and Seabrook had desired, recommending a congress or convention of the slaveholding states "intrusted with full power and authority to deliberate and act with a view and intention of arresting further aggression, and if possible, of restoring the Constitutional rights of the South; and if not, to provide for their future safety and

[28] R. W. Barnwell to Gov. John A. Quitman, Sept. 19, 1850, Claiborne MSS.

independence.'' The convention attracted little attention and
adjourned *sine die* November 18, 1850. [29]

In the meantime, while Seabrook and Barnwell were working hopefully for the cooperative resistance of at least four or
five Southern states, the tide of disunion ran strongly in South
Carolina. Even before the passage of the last of the compromise
measures the organization of the state into Southern Rights Associations was begun. Late in August the citizens of Richland
district met in Columbia, took steps under the direction of W. C.
Preston, former Nullifier, Whig senator, and then president of
South Carolina College, towards the formation of a Southern
Rights Association, and sent out a circular to the citizens of each
district of the state recommending that they take similar action. [30] During September, October, and November the organization of these associations proceeded in all sections of the state.
The Southern Rights Association of St. Philip's and St. Mich-
ael's (Charleston) is typical. Its constitution declared the object of the association to be ''to organize more effectively the
people of these Parishes in the support of the interests of the
South; to promote concert of action among citizens of this and
other Southern states in vindication of their rights; and to sustain the State authorities in whatever measures South Carolina
may adopt for her defense or that of her sister States.'' It provided for an organziation with a president, vice-president, a committee of finance, a committee of correspondence, and a committee of safety to consider all communications, call extra meetings
and make reports to meetings as they saw fit. It declared that

[29] D. T. Herndon, ''The Nashville Convention of 1850,'' in *Transactions of Ala. Hist. Soc.*, V, 227-233; ''Speech of the Hon. Langdon Cheves,
in the Nashville Convention, November 15, 1850;'' ''Resolutions and Address adopted by the Southern Convention......;'' *Mercury*, Nov. 19, 22,
1850.

[30] *Tri-Weekly South Carolinian*, Aug. 27, Sept. 5, 7, 1850; *Winyah Observer*, Sept. 25, 1850.

the association should continue in existence and persevere in its efforts until the wrongs of the South should be redressed or South Carolina resume the powers she had delegated to the United States. [31]

The members of the Winyah and All Saints (Georgetown) Southern Rights Association pledged themselves not to employ any vessel owned or commanded by persons not citizens of a slave state. [32] The planters in other parishes where coasting vessels were used to carry rice and cotton to market, in St. Helena's, St. Bartholomew's, St. Luke's, Prince William's, signed similar pledges. [33] The Southern Rights Association of Beaufort urged entire non-intercourse with the non-slaveholding states and pledged its members to this program, as far as circumstances permitted, and to all measures calculated to attain the formation of a Southern confederacy, and, failing in that, to "support the State authorities in separate resistance to federal aggression." [34] The Colleton Rifle Corps volunteered its services to the state in case of need, and received from Governor Seabrook this reply: "The people of the South occupy a perilous position. How they may be rescued from it is perhaps a question which the citizen soldier will have to answer." [35]

In the multitude of speeches and resolutions and letters printed in the newspapers of the state the line of cleavage between those who wanted united action by the South and those who wanted independent action by South Carolina began again to show itself. Rhett continued his fiery speeches, willing "from courtesy" to wait upon the action of other Southern states, but ready to urge that South Carolina alone and single-handed take

[31] *Mercury,* Oct. 4, 1850.
[32] *Winyah Observer,* Nov. 16, 1850.
[33] *Mercury,* Sept. 28, Oct. 15, 26, 28, 1850.
[34] *Ibid.,* Nov. 15, 1850.
[35] *Ibid.,* Nov. 9, 16, 1850.

up arms if the other states should submit. [36]   In Georgetown
R. F. W. Alston secured the passage of a resolution instructing
the members of the legislature from that district to vote for separate state action. [37]   The Beaufort pledge looked to the same
remedy.   In the up-country, Representative James L. Orr urged
the dissolution of the Union and the establishment of a Southern
confederacy. [38]   At Pendleton and at Greenville, both in the
north-western part of the state, C. G. Memminger of Charleston
drew a picture for the non-slaveholders of that section of the
desolation and the war between the races that would follow abolition.   He urged a Southern confederacy, and in the event of
submission by the other Southern states, the secession from the
Union of South Carolina alone. [39]

Yet there were some South Carolinians who from varying
motives raised their voices in protest against the headlong course
their state was thus called upon to take.   For the first time since
the introduction of the Wilmot Proviso such prominent Unionists as Poinsett and W. J. Grayson and even Perry publicly
avowed their devotion to the Union and their belief that its destruction was neither necessary nor desirable.   In Greenville,
General Waddy Thompson attacked the measures advocated by
Memminger and declared that the South was not so unjustly
treated by the North as many contended. [40]   Perry issued the
prospectus of a new paper, the Greenville *Southern Patriot*, the
policy of which should be to oppose the popular current sweeping over the state in favor of separate state action and immediate
disunion, and to advocate the union of the South in a Southern
congress for the defense of the rights of the South and the pres-

[36] Speech at Black Oak, Nov. 2, *Mercury*, Nov. 8, 1850.
[37] *Winyah Observer*, Nov. 16, 1850.
[38] *Mercury*, Nov. 14, 1850.
[39] *Mercury*, Oct. 10, Nov. 9, 1850; Pamphlet: ''Speech delivered by
Col. C. G. Memminger......in Pendleton.''
[40] *Mercury*, Nov. 9, 1850.

ervation of the integrity of the Union. [41] Both Perry and
Thompson by their speeches in 1847 in opposition to the Wilmot
Proviso had helped raise the storm which now threatened to destroy the Union or to bring ruin upon South Carolina. Poinsett
and Grayson had a more consistent record behind them. Both
now publicly expressed their opposition to any attempt at disunion. Both bravely justified the compromise measures, declared the formation of a Southern Confederacy undesirable as
well as impracticable, and judged the secession of South Carolina alone from the Union nothing but the wildest folly. [42]

Ex-Governor James Hamilton had a somewhat different
point of view but he reached a conclusion similar to that of
Poinsett and Grayson. In a rather remarkable letter addressed
"to the People of South Carolina" he confessed that he had "no
superstitious veneration for the Union," but he strongly depre-
cated separate action by the state, and declared that the people
of no other state considered the compromise measures sufficient
cause for a dissolution of the Union. Those measures Hamilton
himself considered unjust but not unconstitutional, and he
urged that South Carolina accept them as a final settlement.
Should they not prove such, he said, and should the free-soilers
and abolitionists elect a president, repeal the fugitive-slave law,
and abolish slavery in the District of Columbia, then the whole
South could unite in dissolving the Union. [43]

Even so sincere a disunionist as James H. Hammond was
opposed to calling a convention, opposed to passing any hector-
ing resolutions, opposed to any open breaking ground against

[41] *Courier*, Nov. 15, 1850; *Spartan*, Nov. 21, 1850.

[42] Letter from Hon. J. R. Poinsett to "Fellow Citizens," Dec. 4, 1850,
in *Mercury*, Dec. 5, 1850; W. J. Grayson, "Letter to His Excellency, Whitemarsh B. Seabrook, Governor of the State of South Carolina, on the Dissolution of the Union."

[43] Letter dated Nov. 11, 1850, printed in *Mercury*, Nov. 28, 1850.

the federal government, opposed to any attempt at secession by South Carolina, though he thought that ultimately the state would have to take the lead in seceding. ''In a few years,'' he said, ''no one can say when or how soon, the voice of the South will call us to the lead.'' As to his opinion of the compromise, he wrote thus: ''I think the late acts of Congress constitute good grounds for secession, and I think that the Legislature might so resolve and proffer cooperation with any other seceding State— but without bluster. The error of Hamilton and his set is that they look to mere *facts,* not to the motives of men and the tendencies and objects of measures. There was no *actual oppression* in the Stamp Act or Tea Tax.'' [44]

In October elections for members of the South Carolina legislature were held. Though some candidates were requested to state their views on the questions of calling a state convention, of cooperating with Georgia or any other state that should take redress into its own hands, and, should no state take this stand, of submission or independent action by South Carolina, [45] no very clear line was drawn in the campaign on the question of the action by the state in a contingency not yet realized. In Charleston, the highest vote received by any candidate was given to John E. Carew, senior editor of the *Mercury,* who defeated his opponent for the state senate by a vote of 1961 to 782. [46]

The newly elected legislature met late in November. Governor Seabrook's message dealt directly or indirectly almost exclusively with federal relations. In view of the critical condition of those relations he desired investigations into the best mode of improving the natural gifts of the state, with especial attention to manufacturing. The imminent peril of the institu-

[44] Hammond to W. H. Gist, Dec. 2 and P. S. dated Dec. 3, 1850, Hammond MSS.
[45] *Mercury,* Oct. 11, 1850.
[46] *Ibid.,* Oct. 17, 1850.

tion of slavery caused him to advocate measures to check emigration, increase the value of slave property and encourage all classes to possess it. He recommended the purchase of field pieces, the establishment within the state of factories for the production of arms and munitions, and a large increase in the fund for military as well as civil contingencies subject to the draft of the governor. He proposed that South Carolina receive her share of the proceeds from the sale of public lands as provided for by Act of Congress in 1841 and hitherto declined for constitutional reasons. The governor dwelt at considerable length on the differences between North and South, and the evidence for his conclusion that the South could no longer hope for security of life, or liberty, or property within the Union. He concluded: "The time, then, has come to resume the exercise of the powers of self protection, which in the hour of unsuspecting confidence, we surrendered to foreign hands......While adhering faithfully to the remedy of joint State action for redress of common grievances, I beseech you to remember, that no conjuncture of events ought to induce us to abandon the right of deciding ultimately on our own destiny." [47]

By legislative resolution, Friday, December 6, was designated as a day of fasting and humiliation, on which the clergy of South Carolina should call together their congregations to ask divine guidance for the General Assembly in devising measures conducive to the best interests and welfare of the state. [48] On that day the Reverend Whitefoord Smith conducted religious services and delivered a sermon before the members of the Assembly. The sermon was largely a defense of the institution of slavery, and concluded with the advice that it should be left in the hands of God whether He should be pleased that the

[47] *S. C. Senate Journal*, 1850, 14-30.
[48] *Ibid.*, 32-33.

Union be continued with the wrongs of the South redressed, or that the bonds be severed and new combinations formed. [49] Other sermons delivered on this day were in content and in spirit similar to many of the speeches of the time, and were calculated to fan into a fiercer flame the spirit of sectional hatred. [50]

The South Carolina legislature contained at most only four or five men opposed to disunion. Such was the estimate of B. F. Perry, the leader of this handful. [51] Governor Seabrook reported that there was only one man in the legislature in favor of ultimate submission. [52] Petigru, who happened to be in Columbia when the lower house was debating the question of resistance, wrote thus of the situation: ''I am here in the very focus of sedition. Disunion is the prevailing idea, indeed it is a predominant sentiment.'' [53]

But on the question of the immediate action that South Cacolina should take there was a serious division in the ranks of the disunionists. One party, the separate-state-actionists, was in favor of the immediate calling of a convention to take South Carolina out of the Union in the company of others if possible, but alone if necessary. The other party advocated a more cautious course. While the members of this party never failed to declare their desire that South Carolina ultimately secede alone

[49] Pamphlet: ''God, the Refuge of His People. A Sermon, delivered before the General Assembly of South Carolina, on Friday, December 6, 1850, being a day of Fasting, Humiliation and Prayer. By Whitefoord Smith, D. D.''

[50] See pamphlets: ''Views upon the present crisis. A discourse, delivered in St. Peter's Church, Charleston, on the 6th of December, 1850...... By Wm. H. Barnwell, rector of said church,'' and ''Our Danger and Duty. A discourse delivered Dec. 6, 1850, by the Rev. A. A. Porter, Pastor.''

[51] J. L. Petigru to his sister, Dec. 19, 1850, in J. B. Allston, ''Life and Times of James L. Petigru,'' Chas. *Sunday News*, Mar. 11, 1900.

[52] Seabrook to Quitman, Dec. 17, 1850, Claiborne MSS.

[53] Petigru to Daniel Webster, Dec. 6, 1850, Webster MSS.

if necessary, rather than submit, they worked for the calling of a Southern congress as proposed by the second session of the Nashville Convention and opposed the immediate calling of a state convention. Perry explained that both parties were equally determined on a dissolution of the Union; that one hoped to achieve this by means of a Southern Congress and the formation of a Southern confederacy; that the other, believing no Southern state would unite with South Carolina, desired to call a convention, secede at once and thus force an issue with the federal government which would unite the South, or failing in this, leave South Carolina an independent commonwealth. [54]

While the South Carolina legislature was in session the Mississippi legislature provided for a state convention, the elections to take place the succeeding October. Quitman immediately telegraphed and then wrote Seabrook. His assurance that South Carolina could confidently rely on the cooperation of Mississippi, and the speeches of prominent men in the legislature had some influence, said Seabrook, in "checking the course of the impetuous and unreflecting." [55] If encouraging news for the more conservative disunionists came from Mississippi, that from Georgia tended to confirm the opinion of those who believed that delay would not bring cooperation. The Georgia Convention, in session December 10-14, though threatening resistance, even to the extent of a disruption of the Union, to certain legislation against slavery that might in the future be attempted, acquiesced in the recently adopted compromise measures as a permanent settlement of the sectional controversy. [56]

[54] Pamphlet dated Jan. 15, 1851: "Circular of Messrs. Perry, Duncan and Brockman, to the People of Greenville District."

[55] Quitman to R. B. Rhett, Nov. 30, 1850, Seabrook MSS; Seabrook to Quitman, (telegram) Dec. 3, 1850, Dec. 17, 19, 1850, Claiborne MSS. The letter, dated Dec. 17 and 19, is printed in part in Claiborne, *Life of Quitman*, II, 39-40.

[56] *Journal of the Georgia Convention, 1850.*

In the lower house of the South Carolina General Assembly, consideration of the action that should be taken by the state consumed a large part of the session. Of a large number of bills and resolutions on this question, a number were referred to the Committee on Federal Relations. The others were considered in the Committee of the Whole from December 3 to 16. The debates, participated in by a large number of members, brought out clearly the division between state actionists and cooperationists. [57] The result was a report by the Committee of the Whole recommending the passage of a bill for a state convention. In the meantime the Committee on Federal Relations had reported a bill providing for the election of delegates to a Southern congress, and the Senate in one day of discussion had passed by a vote of 37 to 6 a bill for a state convention. The House immediately killed the bill for a Southern congress by postponing consideration of it until January 1. The next day, December 17, the Senate bill for a state convention to meet in December, 1851, failed to pass the House by a vote of 75 yea and 42 nay, the necessary affirmative vote of two-thirds of all members being lacking. Thus both propositions were lost. The House bill for a convention was then tabled, the vote postponing the Southern congress bill reconsidered, the state convention bill added to it as an amendment, and the two measures together lost by a vote of 80 yea to 32 nay, two-thirds not in the affirmative. Next a bill for a Southern congress, proposed by Memminger, was taken up and amended by adding to it the proposal for a state convention. This left the House just where it had been before, so it adjourned in confusion soon after midnight. [58]

The minority opposed to a state convention had defeated

[57] These debates are given in abstract in *Courier*, Dec. 5-18, and *Tri-weekly South Carolinian*, Dec. 13, 16, 18, 20, 1850.

[58] S. C. *Senate Journal*, 1850, 131-132; *House Journal*, 1850, 131, 167, 182, 192, 196, 197, 207.

that measure both alone and when added to the Southern congress bill. The majority had refused to pass the Southern congress bill without the convention bill attached. Only three days of the session were left and unless some agreement could be reached the legislature would adjourn without taking any step towards disunion. A compromise was made. On December 18, a bill providing for the call of and election of delegates to a Southern congress and for a state convention passed the House by a vote of 109 to 12, and on the last day of the session was accepted by the Senate with only three dissenting votes. [59]

The "Omnibus Bill," as it was called, authorized the governor, in concert with the proper authorities of other states joining in the congress, to appoint the time and place of meeting of this body. The purpose of the congress should be to devise measures adequate to obtain the objects proposed by the Nashville Convention, and to report the same to the slaveholding states. The act provided for eighteen deputies from South Carolina with full power to represent the state, four to be chosen by the legislature and two from each Congressional district by the qualified voters, the elections to be held the second Monday and the day following in October, 1851. It provided, further, for the election of delegates, the second Monday in February, 1851, to a convention of the people of South Carolina, for the purpose of considering the recommendations of the proposed Southern congress and to take care that the Commonwealth of South Carolina suffer no detriment in view of her relations with the laws and government of the United States. It suggested Montgomery, Alabama, as the place, and Jan. 2, 1852, as the date for the meeting of the Southern congress. It left the date for the meeting of the state convention to be determined by the governor, should the Southern congress be assured before the next session of the

[59] S. C. *House Journal*, 1850, 216; *Senate Journal*, 1850, 171.

legislature, and if not, then by a majority vote of the legislature itself. [60]   In honor of the passage of this bill guns were fired in Columbia and Charleston. [61]

The legislature showed the temper of its majority when it elected Rhett to Calhoun's seat in the Senate.   For Governor, it chose John H. Means of Fairfield District.   Means was not a prominent South Carolina leader, but he had taken a leading part in the resistance movement in his district, and had been chairman of the Fairfield committee which in 1848 issued an address to the South advocating the establishment of a Southern confederacy.   In his inaugural address he strongly favored disunion, but urged that South Carolina await the results of the measures suggested by the Nashville Convention, and only when all efforts to unite the South had failed "throw her banner to the breeze and leave the consequences to God." [62]

Several measures preparatory to disunion were adopted by the legislature.   It chartered the South Carolina Atlantic Steam Navigation Company for the purpose of establishing communication between the ports of South Carolina and foreign countries. To this company it authorized a five year loan by the state of $125,000 without interest, on the conditions that the vessels of the company be constructed so as to "make them available in an emergency for war purposes," and that at least two of them be completed within twelve months. [63]   It passed "An Act to provide for the defense of the State," reestablishing militia brigade encampments, and providing for the organization of a Board of Ordnance the duties of which should be to care for the arms, ammunition, etc., belonging to the state, direct the purchase of munitions of war, and secure from a competent military engineer an

[60] S. C. *Statutes at Large*, XII, 50-53.
[61] *Mercury*, Dec. 20, 21, 1850.
[62] *Ibid.*, Dec. 18, 1850.
[63] S. C. *Session Laws*, 1850, 29-33.

examination of and report on the defense of the coast of the state. [64] In addition to some small increases in the usual appropriations for military purposes, the legislature placed $300,000 at the disposal of the Board of Ordnance, and added $50,000 to the military contingency fund to be used by the governor only in the emergency of actual hostility. [65] To provide the money for these unusual expenses, the legislature directed the governor to secure from the federal government South Carolina's share of the proceeds from the sale of public lands, [66] and it proceeded to increase taxes by about fifty per cent. [67]

[64] S. C. *Statutes at Large*, XII, 52-53.
[65] *Ibid.*, 7; *Reports and Resolutions*, 1850, 230.
[66] *Ibid.*, 223.
[67] S. C. *Statutes at Large*, XI, 540, XII, 3.

CHAPTER V

SECESSION ADVOCATED

The weeks following the adjournment of the South Carolina legislature in December, 1850, and preceding the election of delegates to the state convention which took place February 10 and 11, 1851, were weeks of comparative quiet. The small amount of discussion that took place served only to indicate somewhat more clearly the division of opinion in the ranks of the disunionists. No open breach was made, however. The compromise forced by the minority in the legislature was accepted by the state-actionists, but they did not give up their insistence upon ultimate secession. The Barnwell Southern Rights Association expressed approval of the action of the legislature but insisted upon secession by South Carolina alone should the Southern congress fail to meet or fail to act. [1] A meeting of the citizens of Fairfield agreed that the state convention should act effectively before its final adjournment by cooperation if possible, but independently if necessary. This, said the *Mercury*, was the platform on which all resistance men ought to stand. [2] On the other hand, Bishop William Capers addressed his ''Fellow Citizens of South Carolina'' in opposition to the measures on foot looking solely to secession by South Carolina alone. He urged the election to the convention of wise and sober minded men. [3] Petigru replied to this that Union men should not vote at all, but leave to those who thought the work of revolution a good work the settlement among themselves of how, when, and where they would begin. [4]

[1] *Mercury*, Jan. 10, 1851.
[2] *Ibid.*, Jan. 31, 1851.
[3] *Ibid.*, Feb. 7, 1851.
[4] Charleston *Evening News*, Feb. 8, 1851.

The campaign for seats in the state convention was almost
wholly devoid of interest. In some districts candidates were
questioned as to their position on secession, and in most cases
they pledged themselves to vote for separate state action in the
event of the failure of the Southern congress. [5] In many districts there was little difference of opinion between the candidates. In Greenville and in a few other districts, the line was
clearly drawn between submissionists and disunionists or between separate state actionists and cooperationists, the latter
standing for disunion but opposing state secession. In Charleston no line was drawn and popular confidence was more the determining factor than definite advocacy of any specific line of
action for the convention. Several tickets were put forward containing considerable duplication of names, but little interest in
the election was shown. The "ultra secessionists" were reported
to be in a very small minority. [6] In most sections of the state the
very small vote cast indicated either a general lack of interest or
the absence of any contest. In Charleston only 873 votes were
cast where in the preceding October, in a not especially hotly
contested election for state legislators, there had been a total of
2743. [7] From other sections of the state reports indicated a very
light vote, a situation explained by ardent secessionists on the
ground that the people were all of the same way of thinking and
all candidates of the right stamp. [8] Perry, however, declaring
that not one-third of the people had voted, saw in this extraordi-
nary apathy of the voters the commencement of reaction. [9] Hammond thought that the convention had fallen dead, and rejoiced

[5] *Mercury,* Feb. 6; *Winyah Observer,* Jan. 29, Feb. 1, 4; *Tri-Weekly
South Carolinian,* Jan. 20, 1851.
[6] John Russel to Hammond, Feb. 10, 1851, Hammond MSS.
[7] *Mercury,* Oct. 17, 1850, Feb. 12, 1851.
[8] *Tri-Weekly South Carolinian,* Feb. 14, 1851.
[9] *Southern Patriot* (Greenville), Feb. 28, 1851.

at the blow the slight vote would give to Rhett's game to commit the state as early and as deeply as possible before a cooling down should take place. [10] Francis Lieber, then professor in South Carolina College, wrote thus of the situation:

"Yesterday the election for the convention closed and, so far as heard from, the people have shown the greatest apathy. In Richland district—the district I live in—we polled 1400 votes at a late election for the Legislature, at this election where the question is secession or not, only about 800! My friend Mr. Petigru, sees in it a symptom of returning sense. I wish I could do the same. To me this apathy has been fearful. To be passive when boys fire crackers near a powder magazine shows an amazing callousness, which in politics means that the game may be taken in hand by a few trading politicians and a number of reckless editors. But one thing I must state in the spirit of truth, that I find now tens and even hundreds who frankly say that separate state secession would be folly for one a few months ago. Almost everyone is for Southern secession, but we must be thankful for small favors." [11]

Whatever the cause for the small vote, the result was to give the control of the convention into the hands of those favorable to ultimate separate secession by South Carolina. The *South Carolinian* declared the secession of South Carolina a fixed fact, the time, only, left for future consideration, and claimed that nine-tenths of the delegates were convinced that redress for the past and security for the future were *"only to be found in secession."* [12] Of the one hundred and sixty-nine delegates the *Mercury* claimed that one hundred and twenty-seven were for the secession of South Carolina alone from the Union, and that of the minority opposed to speedy action, less than ten were submis-

---

[10] Hammond to Simms, Feb. 14, 1851, Hammond MSS.

[11] Francis Lieber to Daniel Webster, Feb. 13, 1851, Webster MSS.

[12] Feb. 22, 1851.

sionists. [13] The greatest claim made by the other side was that seventy-eight delegates were opposed to secession. [14] One delegate wrote that in opposition to state secession he stood almost alone among those elected to the convention. [15]

Among the delegates chosen were many of South Carolina's leading men. The Charleston delegation was largely a conservatime one. It was headed by Langdon Cheves, who had received the largest vote, and contained such men as Robert W. Barnwell, Senator A. P. Butler, ex-Senator D. E. Huger, Judge Edward Frost, Judge Mitchell King, Chancellor B. F. Dunkin, C. G. Memminger, and I. W. Hayne. From other districts were chosen Governor Means, F. W. Pickens, Maxcy Gregg, and former governors J. P. Richardson and W. B. Seabrook. In Greenville B. F. Perry headed the only Union delegation elected to the convention.

In the other Southern states little encouragement could be found for those who hoped for cooperative disunion or cooperative action of any kind. The call for a Southern congress met with little favor. In Alabama the legislature adopted resolutions accepting the compromise measures as a final settlement of the slavery question. [16] The Virginia legislature took the same position, and appealed to South Carolnia to desist from any meditated secession. [17] To Mississippi, the people of South Carolina therefore looked with anxiety. The situation was thus explained to Quitman:

"In a word, then, nearly every man in South Carolina believes that the equal political condition of the slave holding states is incompatible with the existence of the present Confederation

---

[13] Feb. 19, 1851.
[14] *Southern Patriot,* May 9, 1851.
[15] A. P. Aldrich to Hammond, May 20, 1851, Hammond MSS.
[16] *Laws of Alabama,* 1850-1851, 535.
[17] *Laws of Virginia,* 1850-1851, 201.

—that the present Union and the institution of slavery cannot coexist and that so fixed, determined and progressive is the policy, destructive to slavery, which controls the General Government, it is safer and wiser to dissolve all connection with that Government at once......Will South Carolina be sustained by the sympathies of the people or the cooperation of any of the other slave-holding states? If there is a prospect or chance of this, many of her public men will counsel delay and efforts to attain aid so desirable for success. If, however, there be no such hope well founded, then we will go as one man for secession and leave the consequences to the inevitable workings of truth and necessity on those who ought to be with us.'' [18]

In reply, Quitman wrote that it could not be expected that Mississippi would secede unless joined by her neighboring states and that there was little prospect of even the cotton states taking any joint action. He advised his South Carolina friends as follows: "If, therefore, the people of South Carolina have made up their minds to withdraw from the Union at all events, whether joined by other states or not, my advice would be to do so without waiting for the action of any other state, as I believe there would be more probability of favorable action on the part of other Southern States after her secession than before. So long as the several aggrieved states wait for one another, their action will be overcautious and timid. Great political movements, to be successful must be bold, and must present practical and simple issues. There is, therefore, in my opinion, greater probability of the dissatisfied states uniting with a seceding state than of their union for the purpose of secession. The secession of a Southern state would startle the whole South, and force the other states to meet the issue plainly; it would present practical issues, and exhibit everywhere a widerspread discontent than politicians have

[18] John S. Preston to John A. Quitman, Mar. 4, 1851, Claiborne MSS.

imagined. In less than two years, all the states south of you would unite their destiny to yours. Should the federal government attempt to employ force, an active and cordial union of the whole South would be instantly effected, and a complete Southern Confederacy organized.'' [19]

Such was the theory on which the secessionists of South Carolina proposed to act. The *Mercury* urged that a Southern confederacy could only be formed after decisive action by some state and that South Carolina was the only state which could act with the general approval of its people. [20] One secessionist, a member of the South Carolina convention, thought that the conveniton should pass an ordinance of secession and the legislature put this ordinance into effect by annulling the authority of the United States courts in South Carolina, by declaring the ports of the state free to the commerce of all nations, and by instructing the governor to demand the withdrawal of all United States officials and the surrender of all forts within the state. This he thought would be followed by the removal of the customs houses to ships outside the ports and the continued execution of the revenue laws. In Congress he expected a struggle over the question of coercion which, in the event of the passage of a force bill, would insure the aid of at least a portion of the slave states in opposition to its enforcement. In the last resort, he said, South Carolina had all the chances of war; the blockade could do no more than effect the temporary destruction of the commerce of Charleston, and he was willing to see that city laid in ashes if necessary for a successful defense of the state. [21] Needless to say, the writer of this letter was not a Charlestonian.

[19] Quitman to Preston, Mar. 29, 1851, Claiborne, *Life of Quitman*, II, 123-127.

[20] Feb. 27, 1851.

[21] James Jones to Hammond, Apr. 5, 1851, Hammond MSS.

Rhett rejoiced that a Southern congress would not meet, for he thought that such a body would only counsel submission. He declared that the only choice left for South Carolina was submission or secession, and secession he claimed to be her settled policy. He spoke before the Charleston Southern Rights Association on April 7, 1851, and pictured for the citizens of that city the benefits to their commercial and mercantile interests that would result from secession and the inauguration of a free trade policy by South Carolina. The possibility of coercion by the federal government he declared to be absurd, for that government knew that any such attempt would bring the whole South to the rescue. He assured his audience that either South Carolina would be begged to return to the Union with the guarantee of all her rights or she would be left peacefully alone, soon to be joined by the other Southern states attracted by her prosperity and free government. [22]

Rhett's arguments, however, were not convincing, as the letters to the newspapers from Charleston merchants counting the cost of secession clearly demonstrated. [23]   Other outspoken opposition to separate secession was soon made. In Edgefield Senator Butler addressed the Southern Rights Association in opposition to separate secession which he thought would be peaceful and hence fail to bring in other Southern states. [24]   Representative Orr likewise opposed secession and urged that time would bring cooperation. [25]   Even Representative Wallace, who argued at great length that a Southern confederacy was both necessary, natural and inevitable because of the differences between North and South resulting from slavery, favored delay in secession until the state could prepare herself to defend and preserve her in-

[22] *Mercury*, Apr. 29, 1851.
[23] See letter from ''Utter Ruin'' in *Courier*, May 5, 1851.
[24] *Mercury*, Apr. 12; *South Carolinian*, Apr. 12, 1851.
[25] Greenville *Mountaineer* quoted in *Mercury*, Apr. 9, 1851.

dependence. "The price of the Union," he wrote, "is the emancipation of the slave and a surrender of the fairest portion of our
country to the emancipated African." [26]

None of these opponents of separate secession, however, professed any desire to see the Union preserved. Rather they feared
that separate secession would endanger, if not definitely prevent, the formation of a Southern confederacy. But in Greenville, Perry began to publish the *Southern Patriot* in opposition
to both secession and disunion. Although the prospectus had
been issued the preceding fall, the first issue did not appear until February 28, 1851. Ex-Governor Seabrook said that Perry
distributed gratuitously several thousand copies of this paper
weekly and charged that Waddy Thompson had secured $30,000
from the national administraton for its support. [27] Whatever
the truth of this statement, the *Southern Patriot* did receive
federal patronage to the extent of a contract to publish in its
columns the current Acts of Congress. A copy of the paper was
sent to Daniel Webster and the administration in other ways
kept informed of the situation in South Carolina. Perry was an
able and astute supporter of the cause of the Union. He admitted that the South had been insulted and outraged, but he declared that secession would be no remedy. He pointed out that
secession would separate South Carolina from the other Southern states who had all acquiesced in the compromise measures.
He dwelt at length on the disasters that would overtake the state
in the event of secession, either peaceful or by force of arms. He
declared that the members of the state convention had been
elected with indecent haste, at an unusual period, and before the
people had been aroused to a sense of their danger. He urged
that the convention accept the compromise measures and en-

[26] Letter from D. Wallace to the editor of the Laurensville *Herald*,
Apr. 20, 1851, printed in *Spartan*, May 15, 1851.
[27] Seabrook to Quitman, July 15, 1851, Seabrook MSS.

deavor to secure a Southern congress to adopt a platform on which all Southern states could stand in opposition to abolition. He believed that thus the compromise would be sustained and the rights of the South guaranteed and preserved within the Union. [28]

Perry had established his paper when, as Judge Evans said, South Carolina seemed to be going for secession by default. [29] Despite the work of Perry, whom the advocates of cooperative disunion repudiated, and the occasional speeches of some leading men who were becoming alarmed at the course the state was taking, the secessionists for the time being met with no serious opposition. For three months following the election of delegates to the state convention, there was little agitation of the question. A number of Southern Rights Associations met during this period, however, and declared for separate secession. The great majority of the newspapers took the same position.

In January the Southern Rights Association of Charleston had invited the other association in South Carolina to send delegates to a general convention to be held in Charleston the first Monday in May, the purpose of which should be to discuss the proper mode and measure of redress for the wrongs of the state and to effect a more perfect organization and union of the associations. [30] In the middle and upper districts there was some fear expressed that Charleston, apprehensive of injury to its commerce and the possibility of an invasion by federal troops, was growing lukewarm towards separate state action, and that it was intended to use the Convention of Southern Rights Associations to prepare South Carolina to back out honorably and agree to wait an unlimited time for cooperation. [31] If such had been

[28] *Southern Patriot*, Mar. 21, Apr. 4, May 23, 1851.
[29] B. F. Perry, *Reminiscences of Public Men.*
[30] *Mercury*, Feb. 14, 1851.
[31] *South Carolinian*, Apr. 10; Laurensville *Herald* quoted in *ibid.*, Apr. 1; *Mercury*, May 5, 1851.

the intention, quite the opposite was the result. Most of the Southern Rights Associations throughout the state were in the control of the radicals and sent down delegates in such numbers and of such opinions that the conservatives were completely and decisively defeated.

The Convention of the Southern Rights Associations met in Charleston for a four day session beginning May 5, 1851. Delegates numbering about four hundred and thirty were present from every district in the state except Horry. The first day was devoted to organization. Ex-Governor J. P. Richardson, who was chosen president of the convention, reviewed elaborately but calmly the wrongs of the South, and assured the convention that it was its duty to determine upon the remedy and how, where, and when it should be applied. Judge Cheves was not present at the convention but he sent a letter, which was read before that body, in which he urged that South Carolina should not secede alone and thus separate herself from the other Southern states, but should wait upon them and be prepared to join them when they should be ready for resistance. He warned the convention against attempting to decide for the state the question of separate secession, a step which he declared would unfortunately divide the state into rival and hostile parties.

A committee of twenty-one was appointed to prepare and report business to be acted on by the convention. For this committee, on the following day, Maxcy Gregg submitted an Address to the Southern Rights Associations of other Southern States and a series of four resolutions. The address was written in a spirit which took for granted that the state convention would without hesitation provide for the secession of South Carolina from the Union, and was in the nature of a justification of separate action by the state. Almost apologetically it explained that South Carolina had been anxious to avoid any appearance of arrogance or dictation, had desired to act in concert and do nothing separately or precipitately, and was still prepared to give a trial to any effectual plan which might be proposed by the Southern states for obtaining redress and security without a dissolution of the Union if such were possible. But failing to secure this cooperative action, the address declared that South Carolina could not submit, and must exercise the right of secession, a right that each state must decide for itself when to exercise, though it would remain with the other states to determine whether they would permit efforts to prevent the peaceful exercise of this right by South Carolina. The address concluded: "The gloomy prospect of inevitable ruin, to follow submission, appears to us more formidable than any dangers to be encountered in contending alone, against whatever odds for our rights. We have come to the deliberate conclusion that if it be our fate to be left alone in the struggle, alone we must vindicate our liberty by secession."

The resolutions submitted with the address from the committee of twenty-one formed the platform of the secessionists who were in control of the state convention and of the convention of Southern Rights Associations, and against whom no open and organized opposition of any serious consequence had yet developed. For these reasons the resolutions may be quoted in full. They read as follows:

"1. *Resolved*, That in the opinion of this meeting, the State of South Carolina cannot submit to the wrongs and aggressions which have been perpetrated by the Federal Government and the Northern states, without dishonor and ruin; and that it is necessary to relieve herself therefrom, whether with or without the cooperation of other Southern states.

"2. *Resolved*, That concert of action with one or more of our sister States of the South, whether through the proposed Southern Congress, or in any other manner, is an object worth many sacrifices, but not the sacrifice involved in submission.

"3. *Resolved,* That we hold the right of secession to be essential to the sovereignty—freedom of the States of this Confederacy; and that the denial of that right would furnish to an injured State the strongest additional cause for its exercise.

"4. *Resolved,* That this meeting looks with confidence and hope to the Convention of the people, to exert the sovereign power of the State in defense of its rights, at the earliest practicable period and in the most effectual manner; and to the Legislature to adopt the most speedy and effectual measures towards the same end."

A minority report, signed by only three members of the committee, dissented from the majority report on the grounds that it departed from the proper objects of the convention and raised issues uncalled for by the occasion; and it offered a substitute resolution leaving to the state convention to determine the mode and measure of redress as well as the time of its application, and pledging support to the decision of this convention whether that should be for secession with or without the cooperation of the other Southern states.

Discussion of the two reports occupied the last two days of the meeting. In support of the majority report the chief speakers were Maxcy Gregg, Congressman W. F. Colcock and ex-Governor Seabrook. In opposition were Senator Butler, Robert W. Barnwell, and Congressman James L. Orr. Colcock declared that cooperation could never be obtained because aggression would be so gradual that no clear issue on which the whole South could unite would be presented by any uncautious and overt act against slavery until consolidation and abolition had gone so far that escape for the South would be impossible. South Carolina by seceding should present the issue. If coercion followed, then the South would rally to her aid; if not, then she would continue an independent nation. Butler did not believe that secession would result in armed conflict for that would bring the South to the aid of the state. He feared, instead, that economic and commercial coercion would ruin the state and fail to arouse the South. He was confident that if South Carolina should refrain from secession, the other Southern states must eventually cooperate with her. Barnwell explained to the convention that there was danger of confusing the end desired by South Carolina and the means that might be employed to secure that end. The protection of slavery he asserted to be the end. Secession to secure the establishment of a new government was but the means to this end, and when secession could lead to no new government or only to one exposing slavery to greater dangers, secession should no longer be adhered to as excellent in itself. The question, he said, was not resistance or submission, but the formation of a new government that would protect slavery. For the formation of this government, Barnwell urged that South Carolina wait until the other states with interests equal to hers were ready to join her in accomplishing its establishment.

The speech made by Orr throws some light on the motives which influenced the secessionists, to whom, however, the speaker was opposed. Orr admitted that in the convention and perhaps throughout the state the majority was overwhelming in favor of separate state action, but he asserted that few if any would support secession if they thought that South Carolina as a result would constitute a republic independent of and isolated from the Southern states. Yet such would be the practical result, he declared, if no coercion were attempted by the federal government. As a foreign state, the commerce of South Carolina would be almost completely destroyed, her products would have to pay heavy duties when exported to the United States, and the products bought from the North would be increased in price by the amount of South Carolina's tax on imports. The Wilmot Proviso, he said, had been resisted by South Carolina because it would have restricted slavery and made it valueless in proportion to the increase in its numbers; yet the secession of South Carolina would put the same principle into operation by effectually preventing the exportation of slaves to any of the other states. The argument so far was based on the assumption that South Carolina would be allowed peacefully to secede. Assuming on the other hand that force would be used against the state by the federal government, Orr declared that coercion would take the form of a blockade; a form that would excite no sympathy in the other Southern states on which the secessionists relied. Nor was the commerce of South Carolina sufficiently great to induce Great Britain or any other power to interfere. Patience, Orr promised, would gain the cooperation of other Southern states, either in forcing guarantees within the Union or in forming a Southern confederacy. But five years previous, he pointed out, disunion would not have been tolerated even in South Carolina, and now there was not a Union man in the assembly which he addressed. In the other cotton states the value of the Union was openly calculated and disunion advocated. Though temporarily stopped, there were signs of a continuation of Northern aggression, and the time would soon arrive when South Carolina could rally under a Southern banner at the bidding of her Southern allies.

Despite the opposition of Butler and Barnwell and Orr, the delegates from the Southern Rights Associations were not moved from their determination to dictate the policy of separate secession for the State of South Carolina. The minority report was tabled, the address was adopted with but one dissenting voice, and the resolutions as reported by the committee of twenty-one accepted by an almost unanimous vote. The meeting then formed itself into the Southern Rights Association of the State of South Carolina. It provided for a permanent organization with semi-annual meetings and regularly chosen delegates numbering double the number of senators and representatives from each district. It directed the president to appoint a central committee of nine whose duty should be to promote the common cause by correspondence, by publishing and circulating documents, and by all other proper means. [32]

To the minds of some secessionists the Charleston meeting of delegates had settled the whole question definitely and secession was inevitable. [33] Maxcy Gregg for a time thought that the movement would go quietly on gathering strength until the whole state should be secured, [34] yet he realized the danger of a possible organized opposition of sufficient vigor to cause serious embarassment to the secessionists. To John A. Quitman he wrote: ''I beg of you to withhold any expression of opinion against the movement until you have had time for a deliberate survey of affairs. An expression of opinion by you (even if made in reply to some private and confidential communication. from a wavering leader) against the policy which has been adopted by an overwhelming majority of the meeting just adjourned, might cause some fatal defection. For God's sake, let the resistance leaders of Mississippi express no hasty opinion against us.'' [35] Governor Means wrote, ''There is now not the slightest doubt but that the next Legislature will call the convention together at a period during the ensuing year, and when that convention meets the state will secede.'' What the secessionists expected from the other Southern states the governor indicated when he assured Quitman that South Carolina would lead off, even if she had to stand alone, but trusting that her sis-

---

[32] Pamphlet: ''Proceedings of the Meeting of Delegates from the Southern Rights Associations of South Carolina......'' See also *Courier*, May 6-9, 1851. Pamphlet: ''Speech of the Hon. W. F. Colcock ......'' Barnwell's speech in *Courier*, May 27, 1851. Orr's speech in Charleston *Evening News*, June 2, 1851.

[33] Hammond to Simms, May 24, 1851, Hammond MSS.

[34] A. P. Aldrich to Hammond, May 16, 1851, *ibid*.

[35] Maxcy Gregg to Quitman, May 9, 1851, Claiborne, *Life of Quitman*, II, 132-133.

ter states would unite with her in the attempt to save Southern institutions from ruin and the South from degradation. [36] Gregg made this still clearer when he wrote regarding the course the resistance party in Mississippi should take: "Let them contend manfully for secession, and, even if beaten in the elections, they will form a minority so powerful in moral influence that, when South Carolina secedes, the first drop of blood that is shed will cause an irresistible popular impulse in their favor, and the submissionists will be crushed. Let the example be set in Mississippi, and it will be followed in Alabama and Georgia. Imparting and receiving courage from each other's efforts, the Southern Rights men will be ready to carry everything before them in all the three states the moment the first blow is struck in South Carolina." [37]

The secessionists were more justified in their fear that serious opposition might develop against their schemes than in their confidence that the Southern Rights Association Convention correctly expressed the sentiments of the state and that secession by South Carolina was an event already definitely and finally determined. In the light of later developments the action of the Charleston convention, its virtual dictation of secession as the action that the state convention should take, was a grave blunder. The radicals in control of that meeting were able easily to carry out their plans in spite of the opposition that developed from the Charleston delegation and from Barnwell, Butler, and Orr, but their extreme measures hastened the reaction against their headlong course and forced the organization of a party of opposition. Conservative men, numbering among them most of the ablest and best known leaders of the state, who were sincere disunionists and advocates of a Southern confederacy, were

[36] Means to Quitman, May 12, 1851, *ibid.*, 133-134.
[37] Maxcy Gregg to Quitman, May 15, 1851, *ibid.*, 134-135.

aroused by the action of the Charleston convention to a realization of the dangerous extent to which the secessionists were in
control of affairs and what extreme measures they were prepared to adopt. They believed that secession by South Carolina
would result only in humiliation and disaster for the state and
defeat for the cause of Southern Rights and a Southern confederacy.   Justly or unjustly, some of them at least, believed that
Rhett was playing a game, expecting the majority for secession
to be too small to make secession practicable, yet large enough to
insure the control of the state by himself and his faction. [38]

Both Petigru and Poinsett reported that the Convention of
Southern Rights Associations was followed by a considerable
reaction in Charleston. [39]   During the session of that convention
those who opposed the course that it was to take held several
caucus meetings to consider what should be done ''to arrest the
headlong movements of the Secessionists.'' They decided to proceed along three lines of action: first, to buy the *Mercury*, or, if
that could not be done, to establish a new paper in Charleston to
advocate Southern cooperation and resistance to the North; second, to publish and distribute the speeches of Butler, Barnwell
and Orr and letters from prominent resistance men in other
states.opposing separate secession by South Carolina; and third,
to secure the control of the Southern Rights Associations by the
resistance men as contradistinguished from the secessionists and

[38] On this point see A. P. Aldrich to Hammond, May 16; Hammond
to Simms, May 24; Simms to Hammond, June 9, 1851, Hammond MSS.
It should be remembered that Rhett had defeated Hammond for the Senate
in Dec. 1850. Poinsett wrote thus of both disunion parties: ''Depend upon
it the interests of the slave holder and the slave, the bond and the free
throughout these United States will best be promoted by calming as early
and as far as possible the dangerous agitation which originated and has
been kept up by political Demagogues for their own sordid purposes.''
Poinsett to Edward Cole, Mar. 28, 1851, Poinsett MSS.

[39] Petigru to his sister, May 14, 1851, Allston, ''Life of Petigru'' in
Chas. *Sunday News*, Mar. 11, 1900; letter from Poinsett in *Southern Patriot*, June 6, 1851.

the Union men, and to shape the policy of these associations so as to keep up the spirit of the people without running into revolution. [40] This was action which the secessionists feared despite their assurance that the question of secession had been settled. Seabrook expressed it when he urged Senator Butler to use his influence to assure both North and South that South Carolina was in earnest and that a dissolution of the Union was inevitable unless her grievances were redressed; and concluded, "An opposition party headed by you, Orr and Barnwell, is what many men desire, but which I and my friends dread." [41]

The complete breach between the two wings of the disunionists, though unescapable, developed only slowly for some weeks. Representative A. Burt, upon a request for his opinion, replied that the leading object of secession was to preserve the institution of slavery, and that this object could not be obtained by the secession of South Carolina alone but only by the secession of the slaveholding states and the formation of a Southern confederacy. He expected that the federal authorities would coerce the state in the event of secession and no aid could be expected from the other Southern states. [42] In Charleston, the *Evening News,* with new editors in charge, came out in advocacy of disunion but in opposition to separate secession by South Carolina. [43] The opponents of secession secured another paper in Charleston when the *Sun* was purchased and merged with the *Southern Standard.* On July 1, 1851, the first issue of this paper appeared in advocacy of a Southern confederacy and in opposition to separate secession. [44] But the great majority of the newspapers of the state remained ardent supporters of the policy of separate secession.

[40] A. P. Aldrich to Hammond, May 16, 1851, Hammond MSS.
[41] Seabrook to A. P. Butler, May 12, 1851, Seabrook MSS.
[42] Letter published in *Mercury,* May 24; *Spartan,* June 5, 1851.
[43] *Evening News,* May 27, 28, 1851.
[44] Prospectus in *Evening News,* June 7, 1851.

CHAPTER VI

The Campaign and Election of 1851

Though the Convention of Southern Rights Associations split the disunionists of South Carolina into two factions, though it aroused many of the leaders of the state to oppose the course determined upon by that convention and led to the establishment or purchase of some newspapers to give expression to that opposition, popular agitation which would reopen the question of secession for decision by the fully aroused people was somewhat slow in developing. In the up-country Perry called for popular meetings to protest against secession, to instruct their delegates to the convention so to vote, and to demand that the action of the convention be submitted to the people for ratification or rejection. [1] A meeting in the town of Hamburg, "a nest of Northern Whiggery," Maxcy Gregg called it, on May 31 was the first of these. While urging most strongly the necessity of the cooperation of the Southern states to secure the perpetuation of slavery, the resolutions of this meeting opposed the separate secession of South Carolina as insufficient and utterly inadequate as a remedy for past wrongs or as a security against more threatening dangers in the future. They also called on the people of South Carolina holding similar views to hold meetings in response to the Hamburg resolutions. [2] Though a Greenville meeting on June 2 also opposed secession but made no mention of cooperative disunion, [3] for a month longer the opposition to secession languished.

[1] *Southern Patriot*, May 23, 1851.
[2] *Courier*, June 5, 1851.
[3] *Evening News*, June 12, 1851.

Yet the movement begun by Barnwell, Butler and Orr and by these meetings had its effect upon the people and upon the secessionists. The leaders of the latter were chiefly young men comparatively unknown to the people. The secessionists began to doubt whether the Charleston convention had correctly represented the will of the people of the state and to fear that they would not have a two-thirds' majority in the state convention, without which they thought it would be dangerous to secede. Regarding the situation in Mississippi and the probable attitude that the Southern Rights party in that and other states would take towards the secession of South Carolina, they were more than ever solicitous. [4] To them Quitman sent assurances of the strength of his party in Mississippi and reported that though his state could not secede alone, popular feeling warmly responded to the sentiments he had publicly expressed that should South Carolina secede and the federal government attempt to coerce her, it would be the duty of Mississippi, regardless of consequences, to throw herself into the contest and aid her sister state. He urged that there was no hope of effective action by the united Southern states and that the destiny of the slaveholding states depended upon the bold and prompt action of South Carolina. [5]

Even Rhett, who more than any other secessionist attempted to explain the prosperity that South Carolina would enjoy as an independent nation, expected that secession by South Carolina would force other Southern states to disunion and cooperation in opposition to coercion. On June 28, at a celebration of the battle of Fort Moultrie, he offered this toast: ''Co-operation—our fathers obtained it by seizing the stamps, and by firing the guns of Fort Moultrie.'' Above the assemblage floated

[4] Seabrook to Quitman, June 9, July 15, 1851, Claiborne MSS. Printed in part in Claiborne, *Life of Quitman*, II, 139-143.
[5] Quitman to Seabrook, June 26, 1851, Seabrook MSS.

only the South Carolina flag. The speeches and toasts were violent in the extreme. The future of the Union was thus toasted: "*God help us,* and it shall have none." Gen. John A. Quitman was cheered as the first president of the Southern Republic. [6]

Rhett's toast was quite correctly interpreted by Unionists to mean that South Carolina would secede and force the South to follow her. [7] Thus the campaign in Georgia, Alabama and Mississippi on the right of secession had a very practical bearing on the South Carolina movement. The strength of the position taken by the state-actionists, that secession by South Carolina would unite the South and bring cooperation, [8] is shown by the position of Howell Cobb, Union candidate for governor of Georgia. Cobb denied the constitutional right of secession, but he replied to questions as to what course he would take as governor should a requisition be made on him by the president for militia to coerce a seceding state: "This question may become a practical one......I should endeavor to be the *Executive of the will of the people of Georgia*......I should......recommend.. ....a convention of the people, and it would be for that convention......to determine whether Georgia would go out of the Union and ally herself and peril her destinies with the seceding state, or whether she would remain in the Union and abide the fortunes of her other sisters......But if a collision of arms between the states comprising our glorious confederacy should ever come......the Union would fall beneath the weight of revolution and blood, and fall, I fear, to rise no more." [9]

[6] *Mercury,* July 2, 1851.

[7] John B. Lamar to Howell Cobb, July 3, 1851, *Toombs, Stephens and Cobb Correspondence,* 242.

[8] See pamphlet: "Tracts for the People No. 7. Secession First—Cooperation After."

[9] Howell Cobb to John Rutherford and Others, Aug. 12, 1851, *Toombs, Stephens and Cobb Correspondence,* 249-259.

The fourth of July in South Carolina was ordinarily a day devoted to patriotic exercises. There were bands, parades, public dinners, the reading of the Declaration of Independence, much oratory and many toasts. Independence day in 1851, however, was devoted in all sections of the state not to praise of the Union but to its condemnation in violent and bitter language. Rhett and other fiery orators recounted the wrongs of the South, the injustice and oppression that she suffered in the Union, and vehemently asserted that every consideration of honor and self-interest and self-preservation demanded a dissolution of that Union. As one speaker expressed it, the people of South Carolina had assembled, not as on former occasions to honor the day, but to hear the recital of their wrongs. Toasts were offered with sentiments such as these: *"The Government of the United States —A sectional tyranny, a free soil monopoly of the rights, the treasure, and the territory of the South,"* and: *"The Union—A servile yoke to the Southern States."* [10]

While the secessionists were the leaders in most of these celebrations, in Greenville the Unionists and the cooperationists held their first great meeting in opposition to secession. Before a crowd estimated at four thousand, letters from William C. Preston, Judge John Benton O'Neall, Senator A. P. Butler, Joel R. Poinsett, Francis Lieber and others opposed to secession were read. Waddy Thompson addressed the meeting and B. F. Perry offered the report and resolutions which were adopted. The resolutions were lengthy. They praised slavery as an institution beneficial both to the slave and to the country, and they declared that the people of Greenville would defend it at all hazards and to the last extremity. But secession, they pointed out, would destroy slavery in South Carolina, involve the country in ruin-

[10] *South Carolinian*, July 15, 1851. Pamphlet: "Substance of an Address delivered on the Fourth of July, 1851......by Hon. Richard DeTreville."

ous taxation and civil war, and result in dishonor and disgrace to the state. They looked to cooperation for the defense of Southern rights, and recommended that anti-secession meetings be held throughout the state. They demanded that the convention, "so revolutionary in its purposes and so unfairly elected by a minority of the people of South Carolina," be not convened, and that in the event of its assembling the Greenville delegates vote against secession. The final resolution declared that if an ordinance of secession should be passed and not submitted to the people for ratification, it would "be treated as a nullity by a large majority of the people of the State." [11]   By the end of July a number of other meetings opposed to separate secession by South Carolina had been held, and the definite campaign of the cooperationists thus begun. Except in a very few districts this party had no formal organization.

The secessionists controlled most of the local as well as the state organization of the Southern Rights Association. The Charleston Association, however, was controlled by the cooperationists. Its committee of safety had met regularly for some months after the organization of the association in the preceding October, though with never more than thirteen of the thirty-three members present. It had been active in publishing tracts and pamphlets and had conducted a somewhat extensive correspondence. But soon after the Charleston convention of Southern Rights Associations the committee had ceased to meet. [12]   Nor was a call issued for the regular meeting of the association for July 1, as provided for in the constitution of the organization. The secessionists charged, with truth, that the officers had become non-actionists and desired to abolish the association, and they issued a call for the formation of a new association. On

[11] *Evening News,* July 14, 1851; *Southern Patriot,* July 11, 18, 1851.

[12] Statement of I. W. Hayne, chairman of the committee, in *Mercury,* July 14, 1851.

July 23 the secessionists of Charleston organized their Auxiliary Southern Rights Association. [13] Five days later their first regular monthly meeting was addressed by Rhett. Their platform was essentially that of the May convention of Southern Rights Associations, that South Carolina could not wait for any new issue to be presented, and failing within a reasonable time to obtain the cooperation of the other Southern states, should withdraw alone from the Union. [14]

The opposition to secession was formally launched in Charleston when almost 1200 citizens of that city signed a call for a public meeting to give expression to the views of those who were "in favor of Co-operation for the purpose of resistance to the aggressions of the Federal Government but......opposed the Separate Secession of South Carolina from the Union under existing circumstances." The meeting was held on the evening of July 29. Letters from Cheves, Orr, and Col. James Chesnut, Jr., approving the objects of the meeting, were read and later published. Butler and Barnwell spoke in opposition to separate state action. The temper of the meeting was well shown when it laid on the table by an overwhelming vote a resolution declaring that it would be treason for any South Carolinian to oppose separate secession, if that course of action should be resolved upon by the constitutional authorities of the state.

The wording of the call for this meeting gives in brief the position of those opposed to separate state secession. This position was set forth at length in a series of six resolutions which the meeting adopted. On the platform formed by these resolutions the cooperationists made their fight against separate secession. The first declared that measures taken by the North indicated a deep-rooted hostility to the interests of the South

[13] *Ibid.*, July 22, 24, 1851.
[14] *Courier*, July 30, 1851.

and a settled purpose to deprive the Southern states of their original rank as sovereigns and equals in the Confederacy, and that the inevitable result must ultimately be the entire abolition of slavery and the erection of a consolidated government in place of the Federal Union. The second resolution expressed the belief of the meeting that the time had come when the Union should be dissolved and a Southern confederacy organized, but declared a willingness to try any plan short of dissolving the Union, which the sister states of South Carolina might propose for the restoration of equal rights and for the provision of adequate guarantees for the future security of the Southern states. The third stated that the proper mode of procedure for South Carolina was to make common cause with her aggrieved confederates and to "unite with them in council and action to obtain redress for our common wrongs; 'such concert of action,' according to the views of our own Calhoun, being 'the one thing needful,' whether to save the Union, or if (as we believe) that be now too late, then 'to save ourselves.' '' The fourth resolution read as follows:

"*Resolved,* That in the present aspect of our political affairs we deprecate separate secession of South Carolina from the Union: 1st. Because it is due to our Southern confederates having a common interest and threatened by a common danger, to take counsel with them, and especially with such of their citizens as are known to be our faithful and devoted friends, as to the mode and measure of redress for our common wrongs; and because our precipitate secession from the Union, in opposition to their views and wishes, would seem as if we claimed to be the exclusive champions of Southern Rights, an assumption which could not but be regarded as arrogant in us, and insulting to them—thus, in place of harmony of feeling, and concert of action, provoking jealousies, and sowing the seeds of discord between us and our natural allies, and operating to prevent the

formation of a Southern Confederacy. 2. Because our separate
secession would be eminently premature and unwise at this time,
when we may fairly calculate on the cooperation of other States
at no distant period, since the effect of renewed agitation and
continued aggression by Northern fanatics—results which may
be regarded as absolutely certain, must inevitably be, to bring
up some of our sister states of the South to the same position
which we now occupy, and then operate to ensure the formation
of a Southern Confederacy. 3d. Because South Carolina, by
separate secession, would be placed in the attitude of a foreign
government to the other slaveholding states of this Union, the
effect of which would be, that, under the laws of Congress, prohibiting the migration or importation of slaves from a foreign
country into the United States, we should be subjected practically to the 'Wilmot Proviso,' in its most aggravated form. 4th:
Because in all her public resolves, South Carolina has given no
other pledge—has avowed no other determination, than to cooperate with her sister states of the South in resisting these aggressions; and, finally, because in the present posture of affairs,
to dissolve our union with the South, and thus isolate ourselves
from the sympathies and support of those with whom we are
bound together in a common destiny, would be not only abortive
as a measure of deliverance, but if not utterly suicidal in its effects, in the highest degree dangerous to the stability of our
Institutions.''

While the fourth resolution thus opposed separate secession,
the fifth upheld the right of secession as essential to the sovereignty and freedom of each member of the Union, a right no
longer to be questioned. The sixth declared that the hope of
the South for deliverance rested on the formation of a Southern
confederacy. It also set forth the position of the cooperationists
relative to the action that the state convention should take. It
recommended that the convention devise measures to bring about

a system of concert and cooperation among the slave states in resisting the aggressions of the federal government, and also to determine what relation to that government it should meanwhile
become South Carolina to occupy, and at the same time to prescribe to the constitutional authorities of the state such a course
of action as would "enable them to take advantage of all emer-
gencies, and be prepared for all results."

These were exceedingly vague recommendations for the state
convention. Likewise vague were the avowed purposes of the
Committee of Vigilance and Conference and the Committee of
Correspondence for the creation of which the meeting made provision. The purpose of the former was to recommend measures
to unite the public sentiment of the city and of the state in support of the principles expressed in the foregoing resolutions.
That of the latter committee was to correspond with the citizens
of South Carolina and other states for the purpose of combining
Southern feeling and making it conduce to united Southern action. [15]   The cooperationists, as they called themselves, were better able to fight secession than to propose any definite and practicable plan for cooperative action in forming a new confederacy
or, indeed, for cooperative action of any kind.

Thus formally launched, the campaign against secession and
the counter campaign thus forced upon the secessionists in defense of their policy, soon developed into the most bitter and
most hotly contested that the state had known since the days of
the controversy over nullification. In all sections of the state
the partizans of both factions held mass meetings, barbecues,
public dinners, parades. Orators of the day divided their
speeches between denunciation of the North and denunciation of
those who opposed their particular remedy for the evils suffered

---

[15] Pamphlet: "Southern Rights Documents. Co-operation meeting held
in Charleston, S. C., July 29, 1851."

from a continuance of the political union with the North. The secessionists spoke thus of the measure advocated by their opponents: "Co-operation, The name which makes cowardice respectable, and the cloak which conceals treason to South Carolina." On the other hand the separate secession of South Carolina was termed the wildest folly of self-seeking men, a measure that would result in inevitable ruin and humiliation. The newspapers of both parties were filled with editorials, speeches, and anonymous contributions on the questions of secession and cooperation. Pamphlets by the hundreds were printed and distributed throughout the state.

In advocacy of secession Robert Barnwell Rhett was perhaps the most ardent worker. For more than two months Rhett toured the state delivering speeches in all sections. His arguments did not vary greatly from those given in other speeches that have been considered. He traced the history of abolition and Northern aggression upon slavery to prove his contention that when sufficient free states should be created out of the territories of the United States the institution of slavery would be abolished by constitutional amendment. Furthermore, he contended that in addition to the slavery question the South was oppressed and discriminated against in both the collection and expenditure of revenue, and on these grounds found additional justification for secession. He declared that the secession of South Carolina could have only two possible results: either the other Southern states would be forced to join her in the formation of a Southern confederacy, or South Carolina would maintain herself as an independent and prosperous state. He urged that the only method by which cooperation could be secured was the separate secession of South Carolina. [16]

This idea, that the secession of South Carolina would be fol-

[16] See speeches July 4 in Chester District and Sept. 2 in Lancaster. *Mercury* July 8, Sept. 8, 1851.

lowed by the cooperation of other states, was constantly urged by the speakers and the newspapers which supported the cause of separate state secession. Such was the promise made to the people of the First Congressional District in an address written by William H. Gist, later governor of South Carolina, and issued by the convention of the secessionists of that District: "By this movement [secession] a practical issue will be made, and the people of the South no longer deluded by the politicians will rush to our rescue, and upon the ruins of the old corrupt government will be established a Southern Confederacy, uniting a people by the indissoluble bonds of a like institution and similar pursuits, and commanding the respect and admiration of the world." [17] Congressman Wallace from this district came out definitely for secession as the surest way to obtain cooperation. But with regard to Rhett's other idea, Wallace said: "The separate existence of South Carolina is a phantom of the brain." [18]

Apparently this was a common feeling among the secessionists for there was as little attention paid to this argument as there was great inistence that the secession party was the true cooperation party. Yet even on this point some of the secessionists wavered. Congressman John McQueen favored separate secession before the final adjournment of the state convention, [19] and he strongly urged this policy throughout his district. But he admitted that there was no good prospect that any other state would secede with South Carolina and he thought that no force would be used against the state by the federal government to compel civil war and the complete disruption of the Union. He furthermore admitted that secession would not perhaps at once

[17] *Spartan*, Sept. 18, 1851.

[18] Letter to Auxiliary Southern Rights Association of Charleston, *Mercury*, Aug. 27, 1851.

[19] Letter of Aug. 23 in *Spartan*, Sept. 11, 1851; and Oct. 1, in *Winyah Observer*, Oct. 15, 1851.

realize the "entirely prosperous state of things which might be desired," and he continued in this rather discouraging strain: "If ruin should be our destiny, it is but that which all admit awaits us in the Union, and we should have the consolation, at least, to know we met it on the highway of right and honor." [20] This was hardly an attitude likely to convince many men of the desirability of separate secession.

Other active secessionists were Maxcy Gregg and Governor Means. The governor thought that South Carolina would surely secede, and so expressed himself to the militia of the state which he reviewed during the summer. The *Southern Patriot,* which did not spare some of the secessionists, expressed itself thus regarding one speech that the governor made: "His Excellency gave us a war speech but it was the speech of a gentleman." [21]

The cooperationists entered the contest at a considerable disadvantage. At first they had no newspapers. This was remedied to some extent as has been shown, but throughout the campaign they were opposed by a very great majority of the newspapers of the state. They lacked organization, save in a very few localities, while the secessionists controlled most of the Southern Rights Associations. Furthermore the secessionists controlled the majority of the delegates to the state convention. Most serious of all, however, was the momentum of the disunion movement which the leaders of the cooperationists had fostered; there was a spirit aroused in the people which they had worked to raise, a spirit of hostility to and even hatred of the Union, fostered by years of long agitation and countless resolutions pledging themselves and the people to resistance "at all hazards and to the last extremity." To check the disunion movement, or at least to retain control of it and direct it and yet not counsel

[20] Letter to Charleston Auxiliary Southern Rights Association, *Mercury,* Aug. 27, 1851.
[21] *South Carolinian,* Sept. 5, 1851.

submission and the repudiation of all past pledges, was a difficult undertaking. Between state secession on the one hand and abject submission and acquiescence in the measures which they had indignantly rejected on the other, the cooperationists had to steer a difficult course.

The strength of the cooperationists was in their leaders and in the energy with which they attacked separate secession. Cheves, Barnwell, Butler, Memminger, and the other opponents of the secessionists, were men well known to the people. With some exceptions, of whom Rhett was the chief, the secessionists were men of no great experience in public affairs and comparatively unknown to the masses of the people. Yet Rhett was too radical in his opinions for some of the secessionists. Butler was fairly active in the campaign, making occasional speeches and writing letters to be read at various cooperation meetings. To a less extent Barnwell and Cheves did the same. Burt and Orr were active in their respective districts. But perhaps the most active of the cooperationists was C. G. Memminger who conducted a campaign in a number of districts comparable to the campaign that Rhett conducted for the opposing side. His speeches in opposition to secession were published and distributed by the cooperationists.

The secessionists also distributed in pamphlet form the fiery speech that Memminger had made at Pendleton the preceding October, a speech which concluded with these words: "If, however, other Southern states should refuse to meet with us, and we are brought to the alternative of Submission or Resistance, for one, I say, let us secede from the Union and abide our fate for better or for worse. If we are to wear chains, I prefer that they should be put on me by force. I, at least, will have no part in forging them." [22]

[22] Pamphlet: "Speech delivered by Col. C. G. Memminger......at the Mass Meeting in Pendleton."

When he was campaigning against secession in the summer of 1851 this speech and especially the last paragraph caused Memminger considerable embarrassment. He explained that in urging secession he was unguarded in not including the time element, that he did not mean that efforts at cooperation should be given up in one year, when ten years had been required to secure it for the Revolution. He admitted that his words had not been carefully weighed or misconstructions guarded against, and explained that he was aroused by the recital of the wrongs of the South and "was urging on the mountain population to resist injustice, the pressure of which was less realized where few slaves existed." He declared that the choice to be made by South Carolina was between existence as an independent nation or the adoption of measures to bring about the union of the South. He refuted the contention of the secessionists that the state was pledged to secession, declaring that all her steps had been taken only for cooperation in secession. He counseled cooperation as the course that South Carolina should continue to pursue, and urged that for this course sufficient time should be allowed. First there must be secured concert of opinion, then concert in council, and then concert in action. By pursuing this course he believed that the South would obtain the protection of her rights in the Union or stand alone as a Southern Confederacy. He assured his hearers that such a confederacy would eventually be formed. [23]

Memminger was no more definite in his proposals when he advocated cooperation than the other leaders of his faction. Accused by the secessionists of being no better than abject submissionists and challenged to state how they would secure the coop-

[23] Pamphlet: "Southern Rights and Co-operation Documents, No. 7. Speech of Mr. Memminger at a public meeting of the friends of co-operation in the cause of Southern Rights, held in Charleston, September 23, 1851......" Reprinted in full in Henry D. Capers, *Life and Times of C. G. Memminger,* 204-222.

eration they advocated, the most effective reply of the cooperationists was to attack the policy of separate secession. The secessionists argued that the carrying out of their policy would result
either in coercion by the federal government and the cooperation of the other Southern states in resisting coercion, thus effectively destroying the Union, or in the peaceful existence of
South Carolina as a very prosperous and independent state, an
example to the other slave states of the beneficial results of a
separation from the oppressive Union. They placed the greater
emphasis of their arguments, however, on the prospective cooperation to follow secession.

The co-operationists, on the other hand, contended that secession would not bring the South to the aid of the state, and
they centered their attack upon the idea of the separate existence of South Carolina as an independent nation. Some argued
as did Senator Butler that coercion would not be attempted by
the federal government in a form which would bring the other
Southern states to the aid of South Carolina. Others agreed
with Barnwell that coercion would be applied, that no other state
would even then give her sympathy or aid, and that the result
would be the complete defeat and humiliation of the state. All
agreed that independent existence for South Carolina would
mean only increased burdens of taxation and the ruin of all
classes of the population. [24] Great stress was laid on the contention that the cause for which South Carolina stood was not her
cause alone but the cause of the whole South, that she should not
separate herself from her sister states whose interests were identical with hers, but that she should be content to wait and act

[24] For the argument on both sides of this question see pamphlets:
"Separate State Secession, Practically Discussed......by Rutledge," and
"Southern Rights and Co-operation Documents. The 'Rutledge' Pamphlet
Reviewed......" Rhett's speeches contain the most extravagant asser-
tions as to the benefits to South Carolina of independent nationality.

with them when they should come to the advanced positions that she held.

One further aspect of the campaign of the summer of 1851 remains to be considered. Memminger, when he explained his Pendleton speech as an effort to arouse the non-slaveholders, indicated the comparative indifference with which that element of the population viewed the question of resistance to measures antagonistic to the slave interests. The expressors and the moulders of public opinion who have left a record of their attitude were salveholders or closely allied in interest to that class. To a very great extent those who had no personal interest in the institution of slavery were inarticulate. They had no means of effectually voicing their opinions or their prejudices. They possessed the right to vote, but they had no leaders, and the nature of the organization of the state government, the centralization of authority in the legislature, the absence of rival parties to bid for their support, mitigated against the political expression of their class interests. The extent of their class consciousness would be difficult to determine, though there is some evidence of a tendency towards that feeling of hostility towards slavery and the slave owning class which found expression in 1857 in Helper's *Impending Crisis*. During the summer of 1849 great excitement had been created in the state by the circulation of pamphlets and letters calculated to arouse the non-slaveholding class and purporting to be written by South Carolinians. The newspapers violently condemned the authors of this activity as "that hellish crew who seek to break down the constitution of our state, and destroy the barriers which protect the rights of the poor white man, and keep alive in him the spirit and independence of a freeman." [25] From the small amount of these writings which got into the papers, the following portion of an intercepted letter

[25] *Pendleton Messenger* quoted in *Spartan*, July 12, 1849.

signed "Brutus" and dated at Edgefield, July 10, 1849, may be
quoted: "We have formed an association, for the purpose of
comprehending in it all the non-slaveholders we can confide in,
and for the purpose of producing such a change in public sentiment, as to promote our interests against the oppressions of the
slaveholding power." [26]

In the campaign of the summer of 1851 the character of the
appeal made by the secessionists to the non-slaveholders did not
differ greatly from that made during the preceding years of agitation against the Wilmot Proviso and the abolition movement.
That appeal to passion has already been discussed. On the other
hand there is evidence to indicate that some of those opposed to
secession did not scruple to appeal to the prejudice of the non-
slaveholder against the slaveholder. One newspaper editor thus
commented on the policy of the cooperationists: "In some of the
upper districts, the abolition argument is resorted to by the so-
called cooperation party. They state that the excitement is got
up by the slaveholders of South Carolina for the preservation of
their property, and for the purpose of making the poor man sacrifice his life on the field of battle, while the slaveholder is living
in ease and luxury at home. We make no comments on these sentiments. We simply say, the principles are infernal, and the doctrine is the doctrine of devils." [27] Some idea also of the appeal to
the non-slaveholders made by the opponents of secession, as well
as that made by the secessionists, may be obtained from the open
letter written by one of the latter with the *nom de plume* of
"Candor" and addressed "To the poor men of Spartanburg who
are not slaveholders." [28]

"Why do we hear the North abused and the Union spoken
of as a thing that once existed," he asked. "The answer is, be-

[26] *Spartan,* July 19, 1849.
[27] *Palmetto Flag* quoted in *Spartan,* Oct. 16, 1851.
[28] *Spartan,* Aug. 14, 1851.

cause of the existence of Slavery and the deep rooted hostility of
the North to that institution......Be ye not deceived ye honest
hardworking poor man. I know a number of you think that the
negroes will be freed and taken out of the country, and that then
the laboring poor man can strike for any amount of wages he
cares to exact. This I tell you is a fallacious idea, a mere phantom of the brain—no sirs, the North contemplates no such thing,
but the North intends that we shall not have any of the advantages of extending our institutions—that we shall be penned up-
with our negroes in the Atlantic States and thereby be forced to
free our negroes by self defense without an outlet and keep them
amongst us, or by heavy taxes transport them ourselves, a portion of which taxes *you must pay*—will you do it? If not, we
will be compelled to endure equality with them—we will be
forced to allow them the same privileges we enjoy—because they
will then outnumber us and can make us do just as they please—
they would insist on a right to vote and send their negro breth-
ren to our State Legislature and to the United States Congress—
their children would go to *school* with your children—they would
eat at your *tables*, sleep in your beds and drink out of the same
gourd that you do; yea, they would do more than this, they would
marry your daughters, in despite of everything you could do,
and you will be deeply humiliated at the thought that your
grand-children, those who shall inherit your name and property,
are of *mixed blood.*''

"You are told," the writer continued, "that your rights
are not affected, that you have no interest in Slavery—that you
ought not to fight *for other men's property*, the *rich men's property*......You certainly see that when you take sides against
your own country, your own State, it must tend to the ruin of
every man in that state. They tell you further (and the majority of the non-slaveholders, we fear, in the upper Districts of
South Carolina harbour this idle phantom) that, if the slaves are

free, you get more for your labor than you now get. This is not so; instead of increasing your wages it would diminish them from the present prices of common labor which is about eight or ten dollars per month to one or two dollars per month.''

Turning finally to the question of separate secession by South Carolina, ''Candor'' explained that if such a step were taken by the state, the other Southern states would be bound to sustain her. He urged the non-slaveholders not to vote against secession but to trust the members of the convention whom they had elected and the members of the legislature who had ''thought it the wisest course to hold this convention, in order then and there to secede.'' ''It is true,'' he concluded, ''your Delegates may be instructed and they are *willing* to abide by your decision; but you once voted for them and as they are all high-minded honorable men, and true to themselves and true to you; would it not be better to abide by their decision, rather than have agitation in our midst, when there is so much need of the South being united at this time? These Delegates are as deeply interested in the prosperity and happiness of the State as you are and it does seem to my mind, if the slaveholder can stand a dismemberment of the Union, the non-slaveholder will not sustain much damage by way of heavy taxes from the State.''

It was the contention of the cooperationists, repeatedly asserted, that the election of delegates to the state convention had taken place the preceding February on such short notice and with so little explanation of its object that less than half of the people had participated. They admitted that that election had given control of the convention to the separate secessionists, but they denied that the majority in the convention represented the will of the majority of the people of the state, and they urged that the election of delegates to the Southern Congress furnished an opportunity for a fuller expression of the will of the people on the question of separate secession, and they declared that the election of delegates opposed to separate secession would furnish a manifestation of the will of the people which the convention must heed. [29] Even Perry admitted that a majority in favor of delegates to the Southern Congress who favored secession would mean secession by South Carolina alone from the Union. [30] The secessionists on their part accepted the coming election as the test of strength between the two parties. [31] The days set by the legislature for the election were October 13 and 14, 1851. During September both parties nominated their candidates in each congressional district, and conducted a vigorous campaign up to the very eve of the election. Of the candidates nominated by the secessionists the best known were Daniel Wallace, F. W. Pickens, and R. Barnwell Rhett; by the cooperationists, James L. Orr, James Chesnut, Jr., and Congressman-elect William Aiken.

No one expected that the Southern Congress proposed by the Nashville Convention and the South Carolina legislature would meet. The results of the elections occurring during the summer of 1851 in Alabama, Georgia, and Mississippi indicated clearly the acquiescence of the people of the South everywhere except in South Carolina in the finality of the Clay compromise measures. In Alabama the election of members of Congress which took place in August resulted in a victory for the Unionists by a majority of more than 6,000. Early in September the people of Mississippi chose Unionists from forty-one of the fifty-nine counties as delegates to the state convention. The total

[29] *Southern Patriot,* Aug. 29, 1851; *Evening News,* Oct. 11, 1851; Address to Voters by Convention of Southern Rights and Co-operation Party of the Fourth District, Sept. 8th in *Courier,* Sept. 17, 1851: Address to Voters of Charleston District by Co-operation Meeting, Sept. 23d, in *Mercury,* Sept. 24, 1851.

[30] *Southern Patriot,* Oct. 2, 1851.

[31] *South Carolinian,* Aug. 23; *Winyah Observer,* Sept. 3; *Mercury,* Sept. 9, 1851.

vote indicated a majority of more than 7,000 for the Unionists. On October 7th the people of Georgia elected Howell Cobb governor by a majority of almost 19,000 votes, and thereby affirmed the platform adopted by their convention of the preceding December. [32]

It was to Mississippi that the disunionists of South Carolina had looked most hopefully for aid and comfort. The result of the election in that state was accepted by both factions in South Carolina as proof of the validity of their views on the action that South Carolina should take. The *Mercury* declared that it extinguished the last hope of cooperation unless the state chose ''to cooperate in submission.'' [33]   One of the organs of the cooperationists viewed the Mississippi election as a sure indication of Southern sentiment as to secession, and declared that as each election took place in the South, the evidence became more and more cumulative against the separate-actionists of South Carolina. [34]   Though some of the cooperationists continued to claim that the issue was ''Separate State Secession or a Southern Confederacy,'' [35] the *South Carolinian* expressed the true issue when it declared that the question had narrowed down to that of resistance to past wrongs, and that the only choice left to the state was either to cooperate with Virginia, Georgia, Alabama, and Mississippi in submission, or to secede alone. [36]   This was the choice to be made by the voters of South Carolina when they went thru the form of choosing delegates to a Southern congress that would never meet.

Hammond had taken no part in the campaign but he was

[32] Results of the elections given in *Harper's Monthly Magazine*, III, 557, 694, 840; IV, 120.

[33] Sept. 10, 1851.

[34] *Evening News*, Sept. 10, 1851.

[35] Convention of Co-operationists of Fourth District, Address to the voters, in *Courier*, Sept. 17, 1851.

[36] Sept. 24, Oct. 13, 1851.

bitter enough against the secessionists whom he characterized as "the insane instruments—bent upon butchering in their way the glorious common cause." He was even inclined to think that it might be well for the secessionists to carry South Carolina out of the Union, it being perhaps indispensible for the peace and welfare of the country that the state have her comb cut. Regarding his opnion as to the expected results of the election in South Carolina, he wrote: "I apprehend that the Secessionists will carry the State by a large majority on Monday. They are well organized and much excited and will attend the polls while half of those who would be cooperationists if they were anything, are afraid even to vote lest they get into trouble some way......The other side have the topics and will beat them on the stump with the mobs." [37]

The election resulted in a decided victory for the cooperationists who elected their candidates in six of the seven Congressional districts. They secured a majority of the votes in twenty-five of the forty-four assembly districts, and they cast a total vote in the state of 25,045 to their opponents' 17,710. The distribution of the vote for and against separate secession is significant. The only Congressional district carried by the secessionists was the seventh, in the southwestern corner of the state, the district which Rhett had formerly represented in Congress. Charleston voted 2454 for and 1018 against the cooperationists, a total said to be the greatest ever cast in that city. The secessionists carried all but three of the low-country parishes. In the up-country they carried only three districts, Laurens, Fairfield, and Union, the home of Daniel Wallace. Another basis of comparison may well be used than the geographical one. Including Charleston as one, there were in South Carolina only ten districts in which the majority of the population was white.

[37] Hammond to W. G. Simms, Oct. 11, 1851, Hammond MSS.

The cooperationists carried all of these, and carried eight of them by a majority of more than two to one. There were fifteen parishes in whch the negroes composed from 74 to 94 per cent of the population. The secessionists carried all but two of these, and carried them by large majorities. [38]

The foregoing analysis of the vote seems to indicate that the non-slaveholders formed one of the large elements in the vote against secession. At least one manifestation of their attitude on the election days got into the papers. It was reported that near Cheraw in Chesterfield District thirty or forty men marched together to the polls applauding their leader who shouted, ''Damn the negroes and their masters.'' This incident, said the editor who narrated it, was sufficient to show the feeling already diffused into a portion of the people. Such individuals, he said, were to be found in every community. [39] The same editor also gave one of the very few contemporary analyses of the elements making up the cooperation party. ''They have triumphed,'' he wrote in the bitterness of defeat, ''but they have succeeded in instilling into the minds of a portion of our population sentiments at war with our domestic institutions and dangerous to our future peace. The spirit of war upon slavery has been invoked to fill up their ranks......We have among us idolizers of the Union—men who think it treason to talk of resistance to the federal government; we have among us gambling politicians who would barter away their very souls for profit or place; gentlemen of elegant leisure whose voluptuous dreams and sybaritic ease must not be broken or disturbed by clamors for independence; gentlemen whose hearts and possessions are in other States to be endangered by the secession of South Carolina; and last

---

[38] Vote given in *Mercury*, Oct. 29; *Southern Patriot*, Nov. 6; *South Carolinian*, Oct. 25, 1851.
[39] *Black River Watchman* (Sumterville), Nov. 22, 1851.

but not least, we have among us a class who look with envy and dislike upon all who are so fortunate as to own a slave and who will never under any circumstances lend their support for its maintenance." [40]

The results of the election were well summarized by Petigru in a letter to Daniel Webster: "On the 13th we had an election which turned upon secession or no secession, and the secession or revolution party has been beaten upwards of 7,000 votes. But it would be far too much to set this down as a union victory. The opposition to disunion has been made under cover of the same principles that the secession party professes. The manifestoes of both parties are the same in the main......But the no secession party were joined by all the Union men, or nearly so; the rest refusing to vote. And the practical effect of their endeavors is to put down the agitation, tho they pretend that it is their intention to agitate disunion until all the South is of their party. They are blind or pretend to be blind to the evidence that the South does not join them because they are wrong. ......These are the cooperationists who with the union men have taken the state from Rhett and broken as I think the spell that Mr. Calhoun left." Petigru expressed the belief that, public opinion being so decidedly pronounced against a direct attempt at disunion, it was doubtful whether the state convention would ever meet. He concluded, "May such be the end of such machinations now and forever." [41]

* *Ibid.*, Oct. 18, 1851.
[41] Petigru to Webster, Oct. 22, 1851, Webster MSS.

CHAPTER VII

THE STATE CONVENTION

The victory of the cooperationists in the election of delegates to the Southern congress was acknowledged by all parties to have settled the question of secession for the time being. The *Southern Standard* declared that the election expressed the will of the people of South Carolina "opposed not only to immediate secession, but to secession immediate or remote, unlesss with the previously ascertained cooperation of the other Southern States."[1] The secession papers at first accepted the result as a Waterloo for their policy, placing South Carolina on the Georgia platform of submission without Georgia's pledges of resistance to future aggression.[2] One secession editor thus viewed the result of the election as determining the submission of South Carolina to the federal government: "All the blustering and vaporing, and 'all hazard and to the last extremity' resolutions were idle boastings. ......Messrs. Butler, Barnwell and Cheves have destroyed the armed men which were about to rise from the dragon's teeth sowed by themselves."[3] Most of the secession papers, however, including those which had at first viewed the election as determining the final submission of South Carolina, began to insist that the cooperationists now come forward with some definite proposition to which all but the Unionists and abject submissionists could give their support.[4] The *Mercury* denied that as between resistance and submission the election had decided any-

---

[1] Nov. 8, quoted in *South Carolinian*, Nov. 12, 1851.
[2] *Black River Watchman*, Oct. 18, 1851; *Spartan*, Oct. 23, 1851.
[3] *Winyah Observer*, Oct. 22, 1851.
[4] *Ibid.*, Oct. 29; *Black River Watchman*, Nov. 8, 29; *Mercury*, Nov. 8; *South Carolinian*, Nov. 7; Greenville *Mountaineer* quoted in *Mercury*, Nov. 1, 1851.

thing, and declared that the convention would devise some effectual and decisive plan of resistance. [5]

This demand from the secession papers that the cooperationists take some steps towards the redemption of their disunion pledge was the policy determined upon by the Central Committee of the Southern Rights Association of the State of South Carolina. This committee met in Columbia soon after the election and under the date of Oct. 24, 1851, issued a circular "For Confidential circulation among the members of the Secession Party." [6] In this they reviewed the election and attributed their defeat to the combined opposition of two parties: the first and much the smaller in number and hitherto in power was the Union party, the object of which was adherence to the Union at the expense of whatever submission and degradation might be required; the second, larger and more powerful, was composed of disunion men who desired resistance but regarded the cooperation of other states as indispensable or of such paramount importance as not to justify the immediate separate action of South Carolina. Between these two parties, the secessionists explained, there was a third class which, though professing the principles of the latter party, was really desirous of defeating all resistance to past wrongs. They feared that this class might at any moment bring a sudden and great accession of power to the hitherto comparatively insignificant Union party, to whose benefit the success of the coalition had so far inured. The secession party, they asserted, was much stronger than either of the opposing parties taken separately. "It would have been much stronger than the coalition," they explained, "but for the effect upon large masses of voters, of an ignominious panic. Throughout the State, with every appearance of systematic operation, alarms and falsehoods were covertly disseminated among the more igno-

[5] Oct. 18, 1851.
[6] Printed in *Southern Patriot*, Jan. 8, 1852.

rant class. They were told that if they joined the Secession party, or attended meetings of that party, they would forthwith be
drafted for military service. They were told that they would
be taxed beyond their ability to pay. Non-slaveholders were
told that they have no interest in the question of slavery—and
that all the horrors and sufferings of war would be brought upon
them, for the exclusive advantage of their richer neighbors......
A sufficient number of voters were thus controlled to reduce the
party of action from a great majority......to a minority.''

The circular then outlined the policy to be pursued by the
secessionists. Though preserving its organization that party
should make no demonstration, but should attempt to draw a
demonstration from the resistance wing of the opposition. The
Central Committee urged the propriety of efforts through private
conversations and through the press to arouse a sense of responsibility among the true resistance men who opposed secession,
to induce them to declare what they proposed to do to prove
their sincerity and to redeem the honor of the state. Thus the
secessionists hoped to separate the true resistance men among
the cooperationists from the submissionists before it should become too late. The Central Committee expressed a willingness to
support any measure holding out hope of effectual resistance or
leading to secession which the cooperationists might propose.
''Submission,'' it said, ''is not yet to be contemplated as our
inevitable destiny.'' In conformity with the policy of ceasing
to agitate the remedy of secession and of placing upon the vic-
torious cooperationists the burden of devising the measures for
resistance, the Central Committee decided to postpone the semi-
annual meeting of the Central Southern Rights Association and
await the fulfilment of their policy.

James H. Hammond, though opposed to secession and appealed to by the cooperationists to speak out,[7] had taken no active part in the bitter campaign which closed with the election in October. During the summer he sulked in retirement, bitterly hostile to Rhett and sincerely opposed to secession, but fearful that the only result of the factional fight in progress would be a "degrading submission......under some absurd form of bluster."[8] He had drawn up, however, and had published anonymously in the *Mercury* a "Plan of State Action,"[9] the professed purpose of which was asserted to be to furnish a "plan of action short of actual secession yet decidedly in advance of any step taken by this or any other State in our controversy with the Federal Government—or rather with the People of the North."

The plan was drawn up in the form of an ordinance and had been sent to his friend A. P. Aldrich for introduction into the convention when that body should meet. It was a lengthy document of nine articles. It began with a defense of slavery, and it asserted that as the non-slaveholding states had used their control of the government of the United States to impose high import duties and to arrest the extension of slavery for the purpose of hastening its abolition, and as there was no prospect of any change, "it follows that the existing Union of the non-slaveholding States and the slaveholding States of North America, is and ever will be wholly incompatible with the free development of the natural advantages of the latter States, and their attainment to that position of power, prosperity and happiness to which they are justly entitled." The ordinance then asserted that South Carolina therefore desired the dissolution of the Union and the formation of a Southern confederacy, and only refrained from withdrawing from the Union because she was convinced

[7] A. P. Aldrich to Hammond, May 16, 20, 1851, Hammond MSS.
[8] Hammond to Simms, July 1, 1851, *ibid.*
[9] Broadside in Hammond MSS., v. XVIII; see also Hammond to Simms, *ibid.*

that no other states would join her and because she did not consider herself able to maintain alone a dignified, even if a peaceful, independence.   It then declared that the time would soon
come when other states would join South Carolina, and that in
the meantime there could be no utility in maintaining those relations with the federal government which could be dissolved
without a conflict.   To this end the ordinance proposed the
following fundamental laws to be ordained by the convention:
that South Carolina appoint no presidential electors, send no
representatives or senators to Congress, accept no appropriations
from the federal government, and allow none of its citizens to
hold any but local civil offices in the state under the federal government; that the legislature impose a double tax on property in
South Carolina owned by those who should reside exceeding one
month of each year in any non-slaveholding state or states, and
in so far as constitutional impose a tax upon all products of the
non-slaveholding states imported into South Carolina; and finally, that the legislature encourage manufacturing, internal im-
provements, agriculture, and direct trade with foreign nations.
A note to Hammond's "plan" explained that by it a collision
with the federal government would be avoided yet South Carolina be morally out of the Union, and that when Georgia, Alabama, Mississippi and Florida should come to her position the
Union would be dissolved and a Southern confederacy formed.

At the time of its publication the plan attracted little attention from either party in the state.   With the defeat of secession, however, some of the members of the state-action party
turned to it as a possible program for the state convention.   One
secessionist wrote of it: "Secession is dead and I fear buried
forever.   I am therefore anxious to see any plan which makes
a single step towards disunion." [10]   Other secessionists sought by

[10] James Jones to Hammond, Oct. 26, 1851, *ibid.*

conference and by correspondence to induce Hammond to under-
take the formation of a new resistance party on the basis of his
plan of action. They turned to him, one leader wrote, because
they realized that Rhett's leadership could not give it success
and because they could not trust Butler, Barnwell, Preston,
Chesnut, Burt and Orr. They turned to Hammond, he said,
because of his popularity with the masses, his freedom from any
participation in the partisan campaign which had just closed,
and because they believed he could devise and carry out some
feasible plan of action looking to the withdrawal from the Union
at the earliest moment of South Carolina and the cotton states. [11]

Maxcy Gregg, one of the leaders of the secession party, considered Hammond's plan probably the only practicable measure
to save South Carolina from hopeless submission. He suggested
that Hammond's friends ''should agitate the question at once,
and commence the contest with those of their Party who refuse
to join them in proposing it to the Secessionists as a middle
ground to unite upon,'' and he appealed to Hammond to come
forward as a leader of the truest, the staunchest, the most Carolinian party that had ever existed in the state. [12] From Charleston it was reported that the secessionists, defeated in their favor-
ite scheme, were willing to fall back to the next line to their
own, for which Hammond's plan should form the basis. ''If we
find it formed,'' wrote a member of the convention, ''we shall
certainly fall in shoulder to shoulder with those that are there
and battle with honest zeal. It is the only one that presents
itself short of secession, that can save the State from *hopeless
disgrace*. Though slow, it is sure progress towards the ultimate
object and affords an opportunity to those who have vengeance
to gratify, to enjoy the mortification of the submission men and
the trading politicians who have brought up the State to its

[11] John Cunningham to Hammond, Nov. 10, 1851, *ibid.*
[12] Maxcy Gregg to Hammond, Nov. 14, 1851, *ibid.*

present position and then joined the opposition from personal
considerations—'set the woods on fire and then run away.' '' [13]

Whether these overtures were sincere or not, Hammond was
convinced that the secessionists were generally anxious to fall
back on his plan, but wanted it pushed on them as a cooperation
measure. As to whether or not the cooperationists could be induced to accept it, he was doubtful. He realized that the cooperation party, whose sole bond of union was opposition to
secession, could hardly move without breaking to pieces: ''Like
a crowd collected to put out a fire, it must necessarily disperse
as soon as the flames are got under.'' He was fearful not only
that the ''Union submission wing'' of that party would convert
the whole to submission, but that the resistance party in the
other states, cut to pieces by Union victories everywhere, would
be utterly extinguished unless South Carolina should make some
forward movement and plant there as a rallying point the flag
of resistance and disunion. [14]

Hammond and Aldrich conferred together and decided upon
some modifications of the plan. These involved the striking out
of all reference to a Southern confederacy, and the incorporation
of provisions for the creation of a council of safety to advise
with the authorities of the other states and with the South Carolina legislature regarding the federal relations of the slaveholding states, and for giving to the legislature the power to declare
South Carolina no longer a member of the Union as soon as one
or more of the slaveholding states should declare a readiness to
withdraw from the Union. The most significant change was the
incorporation of a clause expressing a willingness to make one
more effort to preserve the Union, proposing an amendment to
the Constitution whereby each section should elect a president.

[13] James Jones to Hammond, Nov. 16, 1851, *ibid.*
[14] Hammond to John Cunningham, Nov. 14, 1851; Hammond to Simms,
Nov. 21, 1851, *ibid.*

and providing that the South Carolina legislature should not put the ordinance into effect until sufficient time had been given for the acceptance of the proposed amendment. [15]

The idea of thus proposing "Calhoun's amendment," was soon dropped on the ground that it should not be a South Carolina movement, much to the relief of Aldrich who thus expressed himself regarding it: "I am and have always been a disunion man. I do not believe that anything the South or North can do, can save the Union and I would not like to contribute anything towards saving it if I could. Yet for the sake of effecting the union of the South I have forced myself to say, that I would lend my aid in carrying out a scheme to prevent disunion." [16]

The secessionists took a more favorable attitude towards the plan of state action than did the cooperationists. Both Hammond and Aldrich wrote to the Charleston leaders of the latter party but got little encouragement for the plan. Hayne thought that to urge it would only produce new distractions, and that no very decisive step should be taken. "The occasion has been lost," he said, "and cannot be recovered." [17] Barnwell found the situation of the cooperationists as a party very embarrassing. He believed that no step looking to separate secession should be taken, but he recommended a speedy reconciliation with the secessionists in order to get rid of the Unionists. The *Standard* took ground against the "plan," and the *Mercury* fought shy of it. Aldrich, however, for the time being at least, believed that a resistance party that would still maintain South Carolina in a position of defiance could be formed from the secession party and the resistance men among the cooperationists. He emphatically declared, however, that he would never act with a party

[15] A. P. Aldrich to Hammond, Nov. 8, 1851; draft of proposed changes, Hammond MSS.

[16] Aldrich to Hammond, Nov. 11, 1851, *ibid.*

[17] I. W. Hayne to Hammond, Nov. 9, 1851, *ibid.*

with Rhett as its leader and the *Mercury* as its exponent. "If Rhett takes any part in a movement," he wrote, "it is half dead the moment he touches it and whole dead when he embraces it. If the *Mercury* supports a measure it is suspected from one end of the South to the other and we must get rid of both." [18]

The position of the cooperation party was embarassing, as Barnwell said. It had recently defeated the secessionists, but it possessed only a minority of the members of both the legislature and the state convention. It had defeated the secessionists on the professed platform of cooperative disunion and the secessionists were demanding what steps would be taken by the victors to carry out their pledges. Early in November some of the leaders of the cooperationists held a caucus in Charleston to determine upon their policy, but came to no decision, save to meet again during the session of the legislature. [19]

On November 25th the caucus of cooperationists from all sections of the state met in Columbia. The confidential circular which the secessionists had sent out late in October was read and created much excitement and a great distrust of Gregg and other secession leaders. It rendered hopeless the idea which Aldrich and some cooperationists had held that the secessionists were in earnest in taking up any plan proposed by their opponents and acting with them under their organization. The cooperationists suspected that a game might be played upon them, confusion thrown into their ranks, and under pressure of excitement secession forced upon the convention at the last moment. Hammond's plan met with little favor. On the question of calling the state convention, a decision incumbent upon the legislature, there was considerable division of sentiment, though the majority, influenced chiefly by fear of what the secession majority might do with that convention, preferred that it should never

[18] Aldrich to Hammond, Nov. 10, 11, 1851, *ibid.*
[19] Aldrich to Hammond, Nov. 11, 1851, *ibid.*

meet. [20]   Unable or unwilling to agree upon any definite policy the caucus adjourned after declaring it inexpedient in view of the existing aspect of affairs to do more than indicate in a series of resolutions the platform on which, in the judgment of the caucus, the people of South Carolina had placed themselves by the recent election.

These resolutions asserted that the state had decided that while the right of secession was fundamental and indispensable, its exercise by a single state without the assurance of support and the concurrence of other states was not an appropriate remedy for existing grievances nor sufficient safeguard against those which menaced in the future, and that any attempt to accomplish this would be in contravention of the clear declaration of public will.   The second resolution declared that the people of South Carolina had decided that concert of action among the slaveholding states was essential as a remedy for existing evils and as a protection against impending evils, and ''that cooperation for these purposes ought to be earnestly sought after and promoted.''   The third, that South Carolina maintained a deep sense of her grievances and dangers and persevered in her determination to remove and avert them as soon as the cooperation of other states should give her action efficiency and render her security permanent.   The two final resolutions recommended the preservation of the organization of those who desired to promote cooperation, and invited all parties to unite in pursuing this policy which the state had marked out. [21]

Perry, of course, was not invited to attend the caucus of the cooperationists with whom he had fought shoulder to shoulder against secession.   That measure defeated, he desired no further agitation of the question of resistance.   He was in Columbia as a

[20] Aldrich to Hammond, Nov. 26, 28, 1851, *ibid.*
[21] *Mercury,* Dec. 2; *South Carolinian,* Dec. 2, 1851.

member of the legislature late in November and wrote thus regarding some of his former allies: "I am afraid there is a disposition on the part of the co-operation leaders to keep up a fuss and excitement. If so, I shall turn our battery against them and assist any forces that may be in the field, whether secessionists or not, in demolishing them, and giving quiet to our country. The rank and file of the co-operation party are decidedly for repose, and will ultimately become good union men once more." [22]

Such was the fear of many secession and some co-operation leaders, but efforts to effect a union of their forces were fruitless. The former charged that the majority of the cooperationists were union men and submissionists. [23] Even the resistance men among the cooperationists were suspicious of the plans of the secessionists. They insisted that their defeated opponents not only acknowledge for the time that secession was hopeless but give it up as the policy of the state for existing grievances. The secessionists refusing to give up their cherished principle and accepting Hammond's plan only as a step towards ultimate secession and not, as Aldrich explained it to them, as a means to the establishment of a Southern confederacy, not a single co-operation leader was willing to lift a finger in aid of the formation of any effective resistance organization. [24] Hammond urged the necessity of the secessionists abandoning the policy of secession forever to prevent the creation of a union-submission party. The secessionists, however, were in no temper for a renunciation of faith and did not think that they should be required to give up more than the idea of secession under existing circumstances. For the time being no understanding could be reached. Gregg well expressed the feeling of some secessionists, at least, when he later wrote: "But if I consented to renounce

[22] *Southern Patriot*, Dec. 4, 1851.
[23] Lewis M. Ayer, Jr., to Hammond, Dec. 1, 1851, Hammond MSS.
[24] Aldrich to Hammond, Dec. 9, 1851, *ibid.*

the right of secession—or what comes to the same thing—to declare that it must never be exercised separately, I should feel that I was abandoning the political faith of my whole life and turning consolidationist. A consolidation with Georgia and Tennessee I regard only not quite so great an evil as a consolidation with New York and Ohio.'' [25]

The cooperationists came to no determination as to what should be their attitude towards the calling of the state convention. It will be remembered that the act providing for the election of delegates to a state convention had not set a date for its assembling. It now devolved upon the legislature which met in November, 1851, to determine whether or not the convention should meet, and if so, on what date. A bill calling the convention to meet on the fourth Monday in April, 1852, [26] was introduced by the secessionists and adopted by the legislature. Party lines were split on the question but the bill passed without serious opposition. [27]

With the definite calling of the convention nothing remained to be done by the politicians and editors but to consider what the convention should do. And very little of this apparently was done. Perry feared that the convention might do some mischief and regretted that it had been called, but since it was to meet he thought that it should lay down a platform broad enough for the whole South and show that the state was ready to cooperate whenever necessary in defending her institutions and maintaining equal rights in the Union. [28] The *Southern Standard* was rather fearful that the convention in the control of the secessionists might adopt some measures which would hasten or in-

[25] Maxcy Gregg to Hammond, Mar. 29, 1852, *ibid.*

[26] *S. C. Statutes at Large,* XII, 100.

[27] *Mercury,* Dec. 9, 1851. Debates summarized in *South Carolinian,* Dec. 6, 8, 1851.

[28] *Southern Patriot,* Jan. 8, 1852.

duce the measures of that party, and it thought that the convention should do nothing, not even make pledges as to what the state would do in the future. [29]   The secessionists were quiet, but as the time for the meeting of the convention drew near there was some discussion as to what it might accomplish.   Everyone accepted the question of secession as dead.   Both Congressman J. A. Woodward and Congressman Daniel Wallace urged in public letters that the chief duty. of the convention was to restore harmony to the state and place the people of South Carolina where the legislature of 1850 found them, united on the State Rights Republican platform. [30]

The idea of reconciliation met with a considerable degree of favor.   The *South Carolinian* reported that the idea was being preached, and declared that the secessionists were willing for harmony on an honorable basis—on any basis of union which did not involve ''desertion of state rights; or the merging of state sovereignty into the consolidation of section.'' [31]   One reason for this desire for a reunion of parties was the fear of the growing power of the Union party in South Carolina.   One journal thought that the convention could do much towards putting down this party and keeping up the spirit of opposition to the Union so that when the time should come for the South to dissolve the Union, South Carolina could be among the foremost. [32]   There were some among the secessionists, however, who still thought that though the convention should not secede, it ought to take some definite action short of secession, by which State Rights and Sovereignty would be ''practically asserted.''

[29] Quoted in *Southern Patriot*, Feb. 12, 1852.

[30] J. A. Woodward to Samuel G. Barkley, Mar. 16, *Black River Watchman*, Apr. 3, 1852; D. Wallace to James Farrow, Apr. 12, *Mercury*, Apr. 16, 1852.

[31] Apr. 24, 1852.

[32] *Unionville Journal* quoted in *South Carolinian*, Apr. 6, 1852.

Among these propositions were the following: withdraw the
state's representation in Congress, abstain from presidential
elections, and ordain prospective secession. [33] Gregg still favored
a modification of Hammond's plan, but even Aldrich among the
cooperationists had given it up. [34]

On April 26, 1852, the convention, elected fourteen months
previously and controlled by the secessionists, met in Columbia.
In accordance with long established custom Governor John H.
Means was chosen president of the convention. The governor
urged that the first duty of the convention was to heal the divis-
ions in the state. "We meet together as members of one common
family," he said, "whose interest, honor, and destiny are the
same. A deep devotion to our country and its institutions should
be the polar star to guide us in our course. The arm of our state,
which was recently strong and ready to strike, has been para-
lized alone by our dissensions. Let us heal them at once, that
with firm and united strength we may meet the enemies of our
institutions. Upon *the union* of our state, I solemnly believe, depends our *destiny*." [35]

Most of the work was done outside of the convention proper,
in party caucus, or in the committee of twenty-one which
was appointed to consider and report upon the act which
had provided for the convention. This committee, with
Langdon Cheves, the most influential member of the convention, as chairman, was composed of twelve cooperationists,
eight secessionists and one unionist. Cheves was very much
afraid of the convention, which he called "an infernal machine,"
and was anxious to adjourn as quickly as possible. Effectual
measures were taken to prevent discussion on the floor of the

---

[33] Correspondent of *Mercury*, Columbia, Apr. 26, in *Mercury*, Apr. 28,
1852.

[34] Aldrich to Hammond, Apr. 20, 1852, Hammond MSS.

[35] Journal of the State Convention of South Carolina, 9-10.

convention by adopting a rule that motions to adjourn, to lay
on the table, to adjourn a debate, etc., should be decided without
debate after such short conversations as the president might
permit. [36]

Thought possessed of a majority in the convention, the secessionists were reported to be in a snarl and to have no
concert or policy. They requested of the cooperationists the appointment of a committee of conference to consult with them and
consider what measures the convention could harmoniously
adopt. The cooperationists accepted and proposed at the first
meeting of the conference that the convention affirm the right of
secession, and state that thought the causes were sufficient to divide the Union, South Carolina withheld her hand for want of
aid from her sister states, but would be ready to leave the Union
when any one or more states were ready to take the lead. The
secessionists rejected this, and proposed, though not unanimously, that the convention withdraw the delegaton from Congress,
refuse to go into the presidential election, and ultimately upon
some contingency, no matter what, secede. No compromise could
be reached and the conference broke up in confusion. The secessionists caucused again and it was reported that they had decided to support an amendment to the constitution giving to the
legislature the right to withdraw the state from the Union by a
two-thirds' vote. Evidently this also was unacceptable to the
cooperationists, for at another caucus of the secessionists those
who desired conciliation and harmony for the state rejected all
violent measures that had been proposed and decided to support
the position of the cooperationists. Rhett was present at this
caucus of his party, though he was not a member of the convention, but a motion proposed by Gregg requesting him to address

[36] *Ibid.*, 13, 14; editorial correspondence of the *Southern Patriot*, May
6, 1852; Aldrich to Hammond, May 3, 1852, Hammond MSS.

the meeting was not accepted. [37]   This was a severe rebuke from
his party.

On the floor of the convention a proposition, in which R. B.
Rhett manifested great interest and which was made by his
brother Edmund Rhett, to nullify the provision of the Constitution of the United States that ''the citizens of each State shall
be entitled to all the privileges and immunities of citizens of the
several states,'' so far as regards the citizens of Massachusetts
and Vermont, and making it the duty of the legislature to prevent the citizens of those states entering, abiding, or holding property within South Carolina, was decisively rejected. [38]   The
proposal to give the legislature the right to withdraw the state
from the Union was defeated by a vote of 96 to 60. [39]   From the
Committee of Twenty-one Perry submitted a minority report,
signed only by himself, which was in effect a denial of the right
of secession, though affirming the revolutionary right of establishing a new government when the old one should have become destructive of the ends for which it was instituted, and which
sought to place South Carolina on the Georgia platform, pledged
to resist future aggressions upon slavery. This report was laid on
the table. [40] The majority report from the Committee of Twenty-
one was accepted by the Convention by a vote of 136 to 19, and
after a five day session the convention adjourned and was declared by the president to be dissolved. The report of the Committee of Twenty-one, representing the only action that was tak-
en by the convention, in the form of a resolution and ordinance,
read as follows: [41]

''Resolved by the people of South Carolina in Convention

[37] Aldrich to Hammond, Apr. 28, May 3, 1852, Hammond MSS.
[38] *Journal of the Convention*, 17.
[39] *Ibid.*, 16-17.
[40] *Ibid.*, 18, 23, 24.
[41] *Ibid.*, 18, 19.

assembled, That the frequent violations of the Constitution of the United States by the Federal Government, and its encroachments upon the reserved rights of the sovereign States of this Union, especially in relation to slavery, amply justify this State, so far as any duty or obligation to her confederates is involved, in dissolving at once all political connection with her co-States; and that she forbears the exercise of this manifest right of self-government from considerations of expediency only.

An Ordinance to declare the right of this State to secede from the Federal Union.

We, the People of the State of South Carolina, in Convention assembled, do declare and ordain, and it is hereby declared and ordained, That South Carolina, in the exercise of her sovereign will, as an independent State, acceded to the Federal Union, known as the United States of America; and that in the exercise of the same sovereign will, it is her right, without let, hindrance, or molestation from any power whatsoever, to secede from the said Federal Union: and that for the sufficiency of the causes which may impel her to such separation, she is responsible alone, under God, to the tribunal of public opinion among the nations of the earth.''

Rhett considered that the action of the convention had determined that the position of South Carolina was submission and her policy cooperation, and deeming himself no proper representative of such a position and policy he promptly resigned his seat in the United States Senate. [42]   Hammond declared, ''The Report and Ordinance are too pitiful for comment.'' [43] But by the newspapers of the state the work of the convention was very well received. Some declared the ordinance a forward step; others rejoiced that it dealt a blow to the Union party; all

[42] Rhett to Means, Apr. 30, May 5, 1852, in *Mercury,* May 10, 1852.
[43] Hammond to Simms, May 14, 1852, Hammond MSS.

expressed great gratification that it had effected the harmonious reunion of the two resistance parties.

Some months later Governor Means reviewed the whole course of the conflict and congratulated the state on the wise and patriotic course of the convention in healing the wounds and re-uniting the state. He thus interpreted the results of the convention and explained the position of the state: "Our destiny, for weal or for woe, is connected with the whole South. Further aggressions (which will surely come) will convince our sister Southern States that the institution upon which not only the prosperity of the South, but Republicanism itself depends, is no longer safe in the Union. Then we may hope that they will rise in the majesty of their strength and spirit, and, in conjunction with us, either force our rights to be respected in the Union, or take our place as a Southern Confederacy amongst the nations of the world." [44]

[44] Message to the Legislature. S. C. Senate Journal, 1852, 29-30.

BIBLIOGRAPHY

In the following bibliography no attempt is made to list all of the material consulted in the preparation of this thesis. It has been thought sufficient to list only that material which has been of direct value, to most of which reference has been made in the footnotes.

I. UNPUBLISHED SOURCES

Claiborne MSS. This collection, in the possession of the Mississippi Department of Archives and History, Jackson, Mississippi, contains valuable correspondence between John A. Quitman and South Carolina secessionists.

Hammond MSS. A large and exceedingly important collection of the letters and papers of James H. Hammond, for many years prominent in South Carolina politics. Library of Congress.

Poinsett MSS. A collection of the correspondence of Joel R. Poinsett, a prominent and life-long leader of the South Carolina Unionists. In the Library of the Pennsylvania Historical Society, Philadelphia.

Seabrook MSS. A small but very valuable collection of the correspondence of Whitemarsh B. Seabrook, Governor of South Carolina, 1848-1850. Library of Congress.

Webster MSS. This collection of the papers of Daniel Webster in the Library of Congress contains occasional letters from South Carolina Whigs.

II.   PUBLISHED CORRESPONDENCE, DIARIES, SPEECHES AND MEMOIRS

Allston, Joseph Blyth, *The Life and Times of James L. Petigru*, in Charleston, S. C., *Sunday News*, Jan. 21-June 17, 1900.
> Very largely a collection of Petigru's letters, occasionally of value for this thesis.

Benton, Thomas Hart, *Thirty Years' View*, 2 vols., New York, 1854.

Calhoun, John C., *Correspondence of John C. Calhoun*, edited by J. F. Jameson, in American Historical Association, *Annual Report*, 1899, vol. II, Washington, 1900.

────── *The Works of John C. Calhoun*, edited by R. K. Cralle, 6 vols., New York, 1854-55.

Claiborne, J. F. H., *Life and Correspondence of John A. Quitman*, 2 vols., New York, 1860.
> Vol. II contains important correspondence between Quitman and influential South Carolina secessionists.

Phillips, U. B., ed., *Correspondence of Robert Toombs, Alexander Stephens and Howell Cobb*, in American Historical Association, *Annual Report*, 1911, vol. II.

Polk, James K., *The Diary of James K. Polk*, edited by M. M. Quaife, 4 vols., Chicago, 1910.

III.   PUBLIC DOCUMENTS

Ames, H. V., ed., *State Documents on Federal Relations*: *the States and the United States*, Philadelphia, 1911.

Congressional Globe, 1846-1852.

Congressional Documents, 1846-1852.

Acts of General Assembly of Alabama, 1847-1852.

Acts of the General Assembly of Georgia, 1846-1852.

Journal of the State Convention, held in Milledgeville, in December, 1850.   Milledgeville, 1850.

Journal of the State Convention of South Carolina; together
with the Resolution and Ordinance, Columbia, S. C., 1852.
Journal of the South Carolina Senate, 1846-1852.
Journal of the South Carolina House of Representatives, 1846-
1852.
Reports and Resolutions of the General Assembly of South Car-
olina, 1846-1852.
The Statutes at Large of South Carolina, vols. XI, XII, Colum-
bia, 1873, 1874.
Acts of the General Assembly of Virginia, 1846-1851.

IV. NEWSPAPERS AND MAGAZINES

Niles' Register, 1846-1849.
Harper's New Monthly Magazine, vols. I-IV.
The Charleston *Courier,* daily, 1846-1852. Charleston Library.
The Charleston *Mercury,* daily, 1846-1852. Charleston Library.
The Charleston *Evening News,* daily, 1851-1852. Charleston
Library.
The *South Carolinian* (Columbia), semi-weekly, Jan. 14, 1848-
Mar. 16, 1849; daily, 1851-1852. Library of Congress.
The *Tri-Weekly South Carolinian* (Columbia), Oct. 2, 1849-
Mar. 28, 1851. Library of Congress.
The Columbia *Daily Telegraph,* Oct. 19, 1847- Apr. 19, 1848.
Library of the University of South Carolina.
The *Winyah Observer* (Georgetown), weekly, 1846-1852. Library
of the Winyah Indigo Society, Georgetown, S. C.
The Greenville *Mountaineer,* weekly, Oct. 23, 1846- Dec. 14,
1849. Charleston Library.
The *Southern Patriot* (Greenville), weekly, Feb. 28, 1851- May
1, 1852. Charleston Library. File in Library of Congress
ending with issue of Dec. 25, 1851, addressed to ''Hon. D.
Webster, Dept. of State.''

The Pendleton *Messenger,* weekly, August 7, 1846- Apr. 7, 1848. Library of the University of South Carolina.
The *Spartan* (Spartanburg), weekly, Feb. 13, 1849- Dec. 25, 1851. Kennedy Free Library, Spartanburg, S. C.
The *Black River Watchman* (Sumterville), weekly, Apr. 27, 1850- May 1, 1852. Library of the University of South Carolina.

V. PAMPHLETS

The Position and Course of the South, by Wm. H. Trescot, Esq., Charleston, 1850.
The Southern States, Their Present Peril, and Their Certain Remedy, Why do they not Right Themselves? and so fulfil their Glorious Destiny. [by John Townsend]. Charleston, 1850.
The Rightful Remedy. Addressed to the Slaveholders of the South, by Edward B. Bryan, Charleston, 1850.
Letter to His Excellency, Whitemarsh B. Seabrook, Governor of the State of South Carolina, on the Dissolution of the Union, [by W. J. Grayson], 2d. Edition, Charleston, 1850.
Speech of the Hon. Langdon Cheves, in the Nashville Convention, November 15, 1850, Columbia, S. C., 1850.
God, the Refuge of His People. A sermon delivered before the General Assembly of South Carolina, on Friday, December 6, 1850, being a day of Fasting, Humiliation and Prayer, by Whitefoord Smith, D. D., Columbia, S. C., 1850.
Views upon the Present Crisis. A Discourse, delivered in St. Peter's Church, Charleston, on the 6th of December, 1850, the Day of Fasting, Humiliation and Prayer, appointed by the Legislature of South Carolina. By Wm. H. Barnwell, rector of said church. Charleston, 1850.

An oration delivered before the Fourth of July Association, at
the Hibernian Hall, July Fourth, 1850. By W. Alston
Pringle. Charleston, 1850.

Our Danger and Duty. A Discourse delivered in the Glebe-
Street Presbyterian Church on Friday, December 6, 1850,
by the Rev. A. A. Porter, Pastor. Charleston, 1850.

Resolutions and Address adopted by The Southern Convention
held at Nashville, Tennessee, June 3d to 12th, inclusive,
1850. Together with a preamble and resolutions, adopted
November 18th, 1850. Published by Order of the House of
Representatives, Columbia, S. C., 1850.

Speech of the Hon. W. F. Colcock, delivered before the meeting
of Delegates from the Southern Rights Associations of
South Carolina at Charleston, May, 1851. Charleston, 1851.

Substance of an address delivered on the fourth of July, 1851,
at the village of Beaufort, by Hon. Richard De Treville,
Columbia, S. C., 1851.

An address on the Question of Separate State Secession to the
People of Barnwell District, by Lewis Malone Ayer, Jr.,
Charleston, S. C., 1851.

Circular of Messrs. Perry, Duncan and Brockman, to the People
of Greenville District, Asheville, 1851.

An Address of the Southern Rights Association of the South
Carolina College, to the students in the colleges, universi-
ties, and to the young men, throughout the southern states.
Columbia, S. C., 1851.

Speech of the Hon. B. F. Perry of Greenville District, delivered
in the House of Representatives of South Carolina, on the
11th of December, 1850, on a number of propositions referred to the committee of the whole on the State and Federal affairs. Charleston, 1851.

Our Mission: is it to be accomplished by the perpetuation of our
present Union? The question considered by the Light of

Revealed Religion in a Review of the Political opinions of some of our Clergy. Charleston, 1851.

Proceedings of the meetings of Delegates from the Southern Rights Associations of South Carolina. Held at Charleston, May, 1851. Columbia, 1851.

Separate State Secession, Practically Discussed, in a series of articles in the Edgefield Advertiser, by Rutledge. Edgefield, C. H., S. C., 1851.

Southern Rights Documents. Cooperation meeting. Held in Charleston, S. C., July 29th, 1851.

Southern Rights and Cooperation Documents. No. 2.—Remarks of the Hon. R. W. Barnwell, before the convention of Southern Rights Associations in Charleston, May, 1851.

Southern Rights and Cooperation Documents No. 6.—Proceedings of the great Southern Cooperation and Anti-Secession Meeting held in Charleston, September 23, 1851. Charleston, 1851.

Southern Rights and Cooperation Documents No. 7.—Speech of Mr. Memminger at a public meeting of the friends of cooperation in the Cause of Southern Rights, held in Charleston, Sept. 23, 1851, for the purpose of nominating delegates to the Southern Congress. Charleston, 1851.

Facts for the People, No. 7. Secession First—Cooperation After. Charleston, 1851.

Southern Rights and Cooperation Document. The "Rutledge" Pamphlet Reviewed, in a series of editorials which originally appeared in the Charleston Evening News.

Speech delivered by Col. C. G. Memminger, made at the Mass Meeting in Pendleton.

Report on the Subjects of Slavery, presented to the Synod of South Carolina, at their sessions in Winnsborough, November 6, 1851, adopted by them, and published by their order. By Rev. J. H. Thornwell, D. D. Columbia, S. C., 1852.

VI. BIOGRAPHIES AND SPECIAL WORKS

Boucher, Chauncey Samuel, *The Nullification Controversy in South Carolina*, Chicago, 1916.

Capers, H. D., *The Life and Times of C. G. Memminger*, Richmond, 1893.

Cole, Arthur C., "The South and the Right of Secession in the Early Fifties," in *Mississippi Valley Historical Review*, I, 376-399.

———. The Whig Party in the South. Washington, 1913.

DuBose, J. W., *The Life and Times of William Lowndes Yancey*, Birmingham, 1892.

Garner, J. W., "The First Struggle Over Secession in Mississippi," in *Publications of the Mississippi Hitorical Society*, IV.

Grayson, William J., *James Louis Petigru, a Biographical Sketch*, New York, 1866.

Hearon, Cleo, *Mississippi and the Compromise of 1850*, in Publications of the Mississippi Historical Society, XIV, 1-229.

Herndon, Dallas T., "The Nashville Convention of 1850," in Alabama Historical Society, *Transactions*, V, 203-237.

Houston, D. F., *A Critical Study of Nullification in South Carolina* (Harvard Historical Studies, III), New York, 1896.

Hunt, Gaillard, *John C. Calhoun*, Philadelphia, 1908.

Jenkins, John Stillwell, *The Life of John C. Calhoun*, Buffalo, 1857.

Jervey, Theodore D., *Robert Y. Hayne and His Times*, New York, 1909.

Meigs, W. M., *The Life of John Caldwell Calhoun*, 2 vols. New York, 1917.

Newberry, Farrar, "The Nashville Convention and Southern Sentiment of 1850," in *South Atlantic Quarterly*, XI, 259-273.

O'Neall, J. B., *Biographical Sketches of the Bench and Bar of South Carolina*, 2 vols., Charleston, 1859.

Perry, B. F., *Reminiscences of Public Men*, Philadelphia, 1883.

Sioussat, St. George L., "Tennessee, The Compromise of 1850, and the Nashville Convention," in *Mississippi Valley Historical Review*, II, 311-347.

Stille, Charles J., "The Life and Services of Joel R. Poinsett," in *Pennsylvania Magazine of History and Biography*, XII.

Von Holst, Hermann Eduard, *John C. Calhoun*, Boston, 1892.